CHOPPER HOBO

SHOVELHEAD DAVE

Chopper Hobo

Print ISBN: 978-1-66783-054-4
eBook ISBN: 978-1-66783-055-1

To All Who Made It Possible.....

I'd like to dedicate this book to the year 1969 which gave us "Easy Rider" and "Then Came Bronson" which inspired many of us to live this special two wheeled life. First up, I'd like to thank my ridin' partner Randal for kicking the 74 AMF Chopper over for me through several states on our road trip in 1979 when my right knee was busted up. Next, big thanks go out for their photographs to Ellensburg Chuck who took the surprise photo for the cover which I never saw until 2020, and to my FB Friend Megumu Karita for the photo of The Rotunda Restaurant.

A Chopper Hobo cannot exist without the help of warm friends who took me in even after knowing me for only a few months. Those Ellensburg friends include Dane & Stacey, Chuck, and Mushroom Tim for allowing me to crash at their homes. Wenatchee pals Taz, Reed, Scott & Bonnie, Jim & Debbie, and Kenny & Darlene for their couches and floors to sleep on.

And a special thanks to my first Bay Area Shovelhead brother, Oakland Steve (1955-1991) RIP who showed me the best of the Bay Area on two wheels, I miss ya Steve, with watery eyes right now, dang it.

Also, a big thank you to the Four Mystery California Choppers who rode up our Main Street and stopped at the red light on that hot summer night in 1967 that mesmerized me beyond belief. You guys will never know how you influenced this 12-year-old punk kid back then.

A special thank you to Mister Richard Sheehy who made all of this possible by finding it on Facebook. He is the brains behind the book so many people asked for. Without him, none of this would have happened.

Last......thanks to my trusty 74 AMF Shovelhead Chopper for never letting me down in 48 years, never coulda done it without you...my best friend. Shovelheads Forever.

-Shovelhead Dave

TABLE OF CONTENTS

Introduction

A true-life account of life of the author, "Shovelhead Dave" At the time a young talented carpenter from Texas, riding his 74 Harley Davidson AMF Chopper, seeking a new life and travelling across the USA.

Dave was recounting his days as a biker living on the road, entertaining a number of "Shovel" enthusiasts on social media, during telling his story many people from all over the world following his recollections have commented it should be a book, so with the help of a friend he met following his stories they have been complied into his first book with more to follow. They are written in his own words, in a style will captivate you and have you laughing your socks off at times with the fortunes and misfortunes of living a life as a biker seeking a new life and looking for employment on his Chopper bike. Through reading this book you can now live it, laugh, cry at the ups and downs of Shovelhead Dave meeting fortune and plenty of misfortune along the journey to becoming the homeless biker tramp living in a tent to become known as the Chopper Hobo.

In the year of 1980, He quits his job in his home town of Dallas sells his house and goes off seeking a new life, travelling across the USA on his custom 1974 Harley Davidson AMF Chopper

This is the true story of the Chopper Hobo......Hold on it's a helluva ride!!

Chapter 1:

"The Night that Changed My Life Forever"

It was the last Saturday of July in 1967. When I tell people this story in real life, they act bewildered and ask me how in the hell can I remember all those details. I say how could I ever forget them? It was the most important night of my life.

Summer of 1967, the Beatles and Rolling Stones were all over the radio and The Mamas and The Papas were on Ed Sullivan and The Summer of Love was in full swing with the hippies dancing in Golden Gate Park in San Francisco. Meanwhile, for me, I was a 12 year old punk kid on the west side of Dallas, hot as hell, sweatin' off my hairless nut bag,. I was a paper boy. I threw the Dallas Times Herald, and that ain't a fun job in the Texas heat, lemme tell ya. I pedaled my bicycle and threw the papers, and at the end of every month I had to go out on the route again with my receipt book and try to collect for my month's work. I had to deal with dead beats. Unless you were also a paper boy, you got no idea how many lame stories the deadbeats can come up with to avoid paying you. And if you got the paper every day, you owed a whoppin' $1.15 for the month, and if you were a Sundays Only customer, then you owed 65 measly cents.

I'd collect at the houses, most people would pay, some would say shit like "Can I give you 50 cents now and the rest next week?" Or the old standard, "My husband has all the money, can he pay you later?"

Anyhow, I had my belly full of them turds that afternoon. so I rode the bike back home to eat supper. When I got about half a block away, the stench from my mom's kitchen was overpowering me and I knew she was in there makin' those nasty

3

fuckin' things she called Salmon Croquettes. She'd open a can of Pink Sockeye Salmon, take them out and roll them in eggs, flour, and corn meal, then she'd stick 'em in the skillet and fry 'em with Crisco. It was gross and she and the ol' man would gobble 'em up like they were the best thing on earth. I had a peanut butter sammith and split for Main Street.

We lived on the west end of Dallas, one block off the old Highway 80 which was Main Street and the old main road going from Dallas to Fort Worth back before they built the freeways. It had 6 lanes, two going east, two going west, with lanes on each side for parking, 30 mph speed limit. It was hot as hell this night and my folks did not have air conditioning. So I headed off to the Wards' Drug Store on the corner. I went inside, pulled some change outta the pocket of my blue jeans which were now cut off shorts, and I made sure to use only the new fake money that was not pure silver, cuz I collected the silver coins. So I put the fake quarter and fake dime in the machine, pulled the lever and my new pack of Winston's fell to the bottom. I walked back outside and leaned up against the brick wall of the drug store, which was still kinda warm from the sun that day. Opened the pack, pulled out a ciggie butt, pulled out my trusty Zippo light,...which I still have today,...and fired up that Winston. I sucked the nice smoke into my little 12 year old lungs and then blew out some smoke rings. I guess I mighta been what normal folks would call a smart ass punk, a brat, a loud mouth, or smart alley kid as my folks would say. And maybe I needed a good slappin', who knows? But I do know this, if anyone other than my folks was gonna slap the shit outta me, they'd better watch out when they leave, cuz I could throw rocks good and could run fast, ha-ha.

All the stores up and down Main Street had their neon signs coming on, the Kips Big Boy Hamburgers sign, Wards Drugs where I was, BC Plumbing, Western Auto, The Uptown Theater had its neon going. I always liked watching the neon signs, that was about the most exciting thing going on for me. And I could tell it was gonna be another one of those boring ass hot nights. I watched the crickets at the corner flying around the lit street light overhead, and the ones that were on the ground would make snapping sounds when the car tires ran over them. How excitin', eh? Yawn.

And then it happened.

I heard a really weird noise coming from the east end of Highway 80, a noise I had never heard before, and I was used to hearing lots of city noises, trains, fire trucks, cop cars, garbage trucks, planes overhead, and ambulances all damn day, see? But this noise was different. I looked to the east and there they were. Four dim bouncy lights, flickering back and forth different ways. This weren't no car unless its lights were getting ready to fall out. They got closer. I stepped right up to the curb to get a really good look. And there they were.

Four of the dirtiest, grime-iest, filthiest, nasty greezy things you ever saw,..... and they were sitting on what appeared to be motorsickles,..... and they came right up to the light which had just turned red. Now if that light had been green and they kept on going, I mighta turned out to be a librarian. But it was red and they stopped right in front of me and changed my life forever. Now my best friend in school had a nice little Honda 90 and he let me ride it, so I knew a little bit,...very little,...about motorsickles. But I knew enough to notice that the two contraptions closest to me did not have clutch levers on the handlebars. I thought that was weird. The greezy nasty things kept making racket. I could see filthy chrome kinda gleaming at me through the grease. I heard the guys yelloing at each other over the racket from the exhaust pipes. The bikes did not have long front ends on them but they did have sissy bars. I knew what sissy bars were cuz the rich kids at school had sissy bars on their Sting Ray bikes.

I was hypnotized for however long a red light lasts,.....20 seconds? Then it turned green and you never heard such a racket when they took off. And then I saw what was on back, California license tags, and they were headed west, I suppose back to California? I have no idea who they were, where they came from, or where they were going. But the impression they made on this 12 year old punk kid has lasted a life time. What would I have ever done without those four guys stopping at that red light that night?

Chapter 2:

SUMMER OF 1979 ROAD TRIP.

My buddy Randal was a Detroit Diesel mechanic in Dallas and he rode a Purple 73 Shovel Chop with suicide clutch and stick shift, sorta like my Black 74 Shovel Chop with suicide clutch and stick shift. Randal and me had a road trip scheduled for the summer of 1979, headed from Dallas to New Mexico, into Colorado, then over into Utah and down to that Four Corners Monument thing where you can stand in 4 states at once, then we'd ride on down into Arizona then cross back through New Mexico to Dallas. We had a week to do it with the 2 weekends before and after that week thrown in, for a total of 9 days.

Then,.....a coupla days before we were to take off, tragedy struck when a fockin' dump truck had spilt some pea gravel down at the end of my street and I did not know it. So I'm ridin' back home on the 74 AMF Chopper after work and I'm downshifting, ready to turn into my street just like I had hunnerds of times, when suddenly, I ain't got no back wheel under me.

That's right, it slid to the left side on the pea gravel and down I went, onto the right hand carb side of the chopper. I tried to save the slide by throwing my right leg out to save the bike, but all it did was throw out my right knee,...bummer. It swelled up and got sore as fock, then it got all stiff where I could not bend it and I could just barely walk on it. I did not go into work the next morning, I sat around the house all day with ice on my knee, hoping it would not fuck up our road trip.

I called up Randal that afternoon and told him what happened. I said I guess the the trip is now off,...sorry. Randal said "Bullshit. We are still going." I asked how? He said "I will kick start your bike for you the whole trip." I was like "Are you fuckin' kiddin' me? You know it's a stroker with high compression, right? You sure you wanna do this for nine days?" Randal said fuck yeah, we are going on the trip. So,....we took off on the trip.

Since Randal was a Detroit diesel mechanic, that means he knew lots of truckers, and those guys had lots of those things you can eat to keep you awake. We gobbled us down some pills and left Dallas after sundown when it was starting to get dark. We rode across the Texas Panhandle on Highway 287 until we saw the sun rise in New Mexico.

I took this picture here up in the high country in Colorado, and yes, Randal kicked my bike over the whole gawd damn trip, ha-ha-ha. He'd kick mine over, then I'd hobble onto it with my stiff right leg all wrapped up in Ace bandages, then he'd go kick his chopper over and we'd take off. Got lots of funny looks along the way.

Chapter 3:

STARTING THE 1979 ROAD TRIP.

We rode through the Texas Panhandle at night to avoid the hot Texas sun and summer time triple digit heat. It was a fun night time ride with hardly any cars out on Highway 287, mostly just the 18 wheelers and us on the two Shovel Choppers. We were in New Mexico when the sun came up, so now it was time to rest a little bit on some picnic tables at a road side rest area.

After relaxing for a bit and letting the vibrations subside, Randal kicked my 74 Shovel over, then I hobbled onto it with my swollen knee and he kicked his chop over and off we went again, looking for breakfast for us and some gas for the chops.

Sometimes we planned road trips down to the last detail. Like if we had a specific destination in mind to get to, like Daytona Bike Week, we would allow so many miles and day and figure out how long it would take to get there. And for those of you old enough to remember KOA Kampgrounds, you might remember how they had their little road atlas things, that had a map of the USA with all their KOA Kampgrounds listed. The beauty of those things were,...say you wanted to ride 400 miles the next day, the guy at the desk could look up the road you were headed, pick out a KOA around 400 miles up ahead, call and make a reservation for your tent site. That was kinda kool in my book. Not exactly the Ritz Carlton, but purdy damn close in my book.

You'd know how far you had to ride the next day to get to your next KOA tent site. And KOA's usually had a little cafe for eats, or maybe vending machines, usually had showers, washers and dryers for your filthy bug guts splattered clothes, and some-times the nicer KOAs even had swimming pools. And I think those KOAs were usually like 4 or 5 bucks a night. If something happened along the way, say a little mechanical trouble, or maybe you took a side trip or maybe had a few too many beers at lunch time and you were running kinda late, well they'd still be holding the tent site for you, so you wouldn't hafta go camp out on the concrete front porch of the high school in Cheyenne, Wyoming like I had to one night.

On other road trips back then, if we weren't doing the KOAs, then maybe we'd camp out in State Parks or National Parks, and this was back before you had to make reservations. You could just ride up and say you wanted a tent site and they'd assign you one. Simple, eh? Those were two ways we used to road trip.

But this road trip was not either one of those types of trips, This was a "Let's Get Wasted Every Day and Have Fun Road Trip." And we did. We didn't care how many miles we were going or didn't go, and we didn't care where we were headed. Our only goal was to have fun getting wasted and riding our choppers in the mountains. That's called keeping it simple.

We were not looking for bright lights or busy cities, we had that back in Dallas. We were looking to get out into the boonies where hardly any people were around. So for some reason I don't remember, we headed to Creede, out on Highway 149, kinda in the southern part of Colorado and a bit west of the center of the state.

This picture here is one Randal took while we were riding up the highway. He had the Kodak Instamatic and turned around and took this action picture, and if ya look really closely, you can see the handle of my walking cane sticking out of the back pack on the back of the chopper.

Chapter 4:

THE FIRST NIGHT.

We left and arrived into Colorado and spent the first night camped out and then headed on to Creede the next day. The next day found us riding through the mountains on Highway 149 going into Creede. Once we got into town we found out it was a really cool little cowboy town. I think its history was an old silver mining town. If any of your folks lived there, traveled there, or know more about Creede than I do, please feel free to correct me, cuz we were just wasted chopper tourists.

We rode up and down the Main Drag and liked Creede enough that we circled the two Shovel Choppers back around and headed back outta town to the southeast end where we had come from cuz we had seen a nice little camp ground on the way into town, maybe 2 or 3 miles outta town next to a river.

So we gave the campground guy a few bucks and set up our tents, then Randal kicked over the two choppers and we headed back into Creede for eats and drinks. We had noticed this one saloon in town that looked like lots of fun, an old cowboy saloon with swinging doors, even. So we pulled the chops up in front of the bar and shut 'em off. The racket from the exhaust pipes attracted a few folks who came to the swinging doors and looked out at us and one guy yelled out "ALLLL RIGHT!" Looked like it might be a fun and friendly place after all. And the town had those old wooden sidewalks like the old downtown part of Fort Worth had. It felt kinda like home. And we saw the town Sheriff, and he had on cowboy boots and a cowboy hat and a brown leather vest and a six point star and a 6 shooter in his holster, just like the old west days.

So Randal started into the saloon swinging doors and I grabbed my walking cane and hobbled along behind him. The saloon was a fairly nice sized place, had a pool table and juke box, had some decent food and cold beer and friendly people. While I normally like to shoot pool a lot, I was gimped up with my right knee being out, so I just watched mostly and my main job was ordering the drinks and playing the juke box.

And then? The Tequila came out.

And next thing we knew, it was closing time, We were drunk as skunks, and didn't really even know where we were. The temperature had dropped a bit in the night, and Creede sits up a bit over 8,500-foot elevation, and that meant the two Shovels were now kinda cold. And that meant Randal had to kick over my cold 84 inch stroker,..... while he was drunk. After maybe 3 or 4 tries, it popped and fired up and the folks at the swinging doors let out whoops of joy, I hobbled onto my bike and then Randal kicked his Shovel over, and we pushed in the foot clutches, the open belt drives made their spinning sounds, we hit the stick shifts into first gear and took off back to our tents while the little crowd was laughing and yelling and telling us good bye. It was a really fun night I still remember.

Although it was kinda cold in the mountains at night, the moon was out bright and it was a fun ride, nice and crisp enough to kinda clear the ta-kill-ya out of our boggins,....sorta. And then? Just as we got close to the camp ground, ol' Randal decided to wind out his throttle and he took off like a bat outta hell. I had no idea what he was doing, and I'm sure he had no idea where he was going, ha-ha-ha. I pulled on into the campground up next to our tents and shut the chopper off. I put the kickstand down, leaned the bike over and just sat there on it for a bit.

I could hear Randal's Shovel in the distance getting quieter, then it got really quiet. Hmm. What happened? Then I heard it off in the distance again and it got louder and louder until he got back to the campground and pulled up next to me. He pulled up in the gravel and shut his motor off.

I asked him what happened. He said he went too far and when he found out what he did, that he tried to turn around in the road, but his front wheel went into the soft dirt shoulder part and he lost his drunk balance. So I asked him "You mean you dropped your bike?" He said yep. He dropped it on the left side, but at least he did not break off a clutch hub stud, so that was good. We laughed about it, since he and his bike were OK. And then it dawned on me what a pile of bullshit we woulda been in if he had dropped his bike on the right hand side and thrown HIS right knee out, bwahahaha! We coulda been two stuck young punk saddle tramps up 8,500 feet in the Rockies with no way to start either chopper and we were about 800 miles from home. Let that one sink in.

This is a picture I took of Randal riding up the road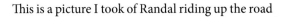

Chapter 5:

GAINING ALTITUDE

We left off last time getting kinda drunkish at the old cowboy bar in Creede, Colorado, staying til the bar closed then riding back to where we were camped out just south of town.

Woke up the next morning with some nice Tequila hangovers, hahaha. Rolled up the sleeping bags and tents, packed them on the choppers, got ready to leave the camp. Randal kicked both chops over and we were off back into Creede for some breakfast for hungover hungry us and some gas for the thirsty bikes. We made it into downtown Creede in no time flat.

We backed the choppers into the curb outside a little cafe/diner. It was a little mom and pop joint, with maybe a half dozen locals inside. We got some strange looks as we moseyed in, kinda like we had just landed a flying saucer out on the Main Drag and were two Martians coming in to eat with them all. They had a juke box, but unlike the one from the night before with old rock and roll in it, this one had old country music in it, which was also fine with us. I hobbled over to it with the walking cane and put some folding money in it and played us some Willie and Waylon, Loretta, Merle, George and Tammy, and other good ol' stuff like that.

The nice little lady was like a grand mom, waiting on the tables and running the cash register while the old guy was the short order cook on the grill. I remember getting some tasty biscuits with sausage gravy and scrambled eggs and hash browns. There were 4 things we ate that stood out to me on this trip and this good homemade breakfast was one of them. I remember leaving the lady a nice 5 dollar bill for her tip, just to let her know all us scooter tramps ain't all that evil. Now 5 bucks may not seem like much of a tip today, but this was back in 1979 when most guys slid a couple or three quarters under the edge of the plate, so that Fiver mighta been the best tip she got all that summer.

Anyhow, we were full, time to fill up the choppers and hit the road for Antlers, our next destination. Antlers was about a 5 or 6 hour ride away, up north and a little bit west of Creede. The elevation of Antlers is a little over 5,000 feet, so it would be a downhill ride, , cuz we were currently at 8,700 feet in Creede.

This photo here was taken along the way, and don't ask me what the hell it is cuz I don't know. Maybe some of you do? Is it an old abandoned mine? A landing spot for UFO space ships, hahaha? Who knows? You can also see in the picture how my right knee is still swollen, even 5 days after I went down on the 74 Shovel in Dallas, and there's that trusty walking cane handle still sticking out of the duffel bag on the back of my chopper.

We rode off leaving Creede for Antlers, Colorado, which was about a 5 to 6 hour ride to the northwest of Creede. Now riding them suicide clutch stick shifting rigid choppers cross country ain't exactly for delicate wannabes and sissies. Even with our iron butts, every once in a while we'd stop to stretch our legs and light up a big fattie and enjoy the clean mountain air,....which we just made smell like devil weed all around us, ha-ha-ha.

This picture is us doing just that......a nice rest stop. We pulled off the road, had a nice view, got a good buzz going, and everything was calm and quiet.... until Randal kicked over the Shovel Choppers again when it was time for us to split.

Chapter 6:

_____

PIGS IN THE DIRT.

So, we are at around 8,000 feet above sea level, leaving Creede Colorado headed for a little place called Antlers that sits around 5,000 feet elevation. It was about a 5 to 6 hour ride through the awesome high country scenery.

We stopped along the way for gas and lunch and some weed breaks. We rode into Antlers that afternoon and it was even smaller than Creede. Ate at a little place there in the small town, had a few beers at the bar and then had to go look for a place to camp for the night. Not only did we not find a KOA Kampground, we didn't see any kinda campground, hahaha. So we kept riding through the mountains with the sun setting and the temperature dropping. When the sun goes down in the high country, it can get kinda cold, even in the middle of summer.

We kept riding through the desolate country, still no campground in sight. But,...we did eventually happen to find one of those Road Side Rest Areas, the little kind with 2 or 3 picnic tables and the big sign that sez "No Overnight Camping." Well what the hell? We've gotta camp somewhere,...right? So we pulled the choppers into the picnic table area that was hidden the most in the back, and we set up the tents and now it was getting pretty dark. Chances are no cop is gonna come our way up here in the middle of nowhere at night,.....right?

Wrong, ha-ha. It musta been around 11 or maybe even midnight, who knows? All we knew was that we got woken up really fast when the bright headlights of what turned out to be a squad car filled our tents with light. Then a voice over a loud speaker in the squad car told us to get out of our tents. So we did. There to our disgust was a squad car with two uniformed goons in it. The smaller older Barney Fife type of guy musta been the boss, cuz he was the one with the microphone yelling at us two chopper bums, who were simply trying to get some sleep out in the middle of the woods where we weren't bothering nobody. The other cop was a younger bigger guy, maybe even about our age, mid 20s, and he was about as big as Jackie Gleason. Anyhow, they told us to leave cuz no overnight camping was allowed. So we said OK and the squad car left.

Randal and me groaned and looked at each other like,......really? OK, the sign said No Overnight Camping, we get it, but we weren't hurtin' nobody, did not even have a camp fire going, we were just there and the cops did not like us being there, breathing their air, hah. So Randal looks at me and I looked at him and we both musta had the same idea at the same time. Randal sez "What if we just move the tents a little further back and hide the bikes more over in the trees?" I said it sounded good to me, so that's what we did. Or well, it's mostly what Randal did for us, cuz I was still hobblin' around on the walking cane, our tents were those little pup tents, easy to move. We yanked up the tent pole stakes front and back, pulled up the 4 corner stakes and moved them back some, then re-staked them. Randal moved the choppers back into the trees some more with the carb and exhaust pipe sides facing back into the woods. That way, there'd be less chrome shining for The Man to spot, see? So we climbed back into the tents and tried to snooze some more.

But it was not gonna happen. What musta been within an hour or so, there were The Pigs again, and this time they pulled the squad car right up to our tents and hit us with all 4 bright lights, left the motor running, gunned their engine like they were gonna drive right through our tents, honked their horn and then started yelling at us over their loud speaker under the hood. "WE TOLD YOU TO LEAVE! NOW GET THE HELL OUTTA HERE!"

Here is another picture from the road side.

So Randal and me come climbing out of our pup tents, all groggy and pissed off that these fuckers had nothing better to do than to make us leave the rest area, probably 1 or 2 AM by now. So there we were, pulling our tents down and rolling up the sleeping bags, in the wee hours of the morning with 2 pigs smiling at us for the fun they were having making our night miserable, I was hobbling around on my bad right leg with the walking cane trying to fold up my tent and bag, and I actually think they thought that was kinda extra funny, watching me be miserable, ha-ha.

We got the choppers packed up for the road. Now,......it was time for Randal to kick them over. On the entire trip, he always kicked my chopper over first, got it running, then he'd go kick his over. Well guess whose 74 AMF 86-inch Stroker with 9.5: 1 compression pistons doesn't like to start when it's cold? That fucker can be fin-icky even with me, and I know it better than any human on earth, hah, cuz I created the bastard. Well poor Randal kicked and kicked and kicked. I had the big 44 mm Mikuni on it back then, so I'd work the choke while Randal tried to get it started. He could get a few pops out of it, but that was all. So I looked at the Head Pig and said "We might just hafta sit here at the picnic table until sunrise, cuz it don't look like it is gonna start up tonight."

The Head Pig scowls, looks at me and sez "Will it push start?" I mean, this pig fucker was determined to get us outta his rest area, eh? So I said "Yeah, it should push start, but it's gonna take more than one guy to do it." So the Head Pig looks at the Deputy Pig and tells him to help push start it, We already had my chopper pointed in the right direction to leave on the dirt road we came in on. So I climbed onto the 74, pushed in the suicide clutch, stuck it in second, and Randal and the Deputy Pig started pushing me. OK, that chopper probably weighs about 500 pounds, my ass was another 200 pounds, plus the road gear was packed on it, too. So maybe it was close to 800 pounds they were trying to push, in the middle of the night, on a dirt road in the cold out in the middle of nowhere, ha-ha.

They pushed, I still had it in second gear, let out the foot clutch,......POP,....and nuthin'. Stopped in the dirt. OK, time for Try Number 2. Here is where it gets extra funny, especially if your are a football fan like Randal and me were from Dallas and were Cowboys fans. This road trip is 1979. Who remembers the 1978 Super Bowl? It was Dallas Cowboys vs. Denver Broncos, hah- hah-ha!, and Cowboys beat the shit outta them Broncos 27 to 10. Maybe that's why these Colorado Pigs hated us sooo much, cuz we had Texas license tags? Who knows?

Anyhow, for Push Start #2, Randal and the Deputy Pig got me going, and then Randal yells out "Let's see what those Denver Broncos are made of!",...and that Deputy Pig got extra huffy and they pushed me extra hard, I had it in second gear and popped out the clutch. And just as the 74 AMF popped really loud through the fishtails and fired to life, I heard this big "OOOMPH!" sound and heard something fall behind me. I had the 74 idling, so I kept goosing the throttle to keep it going and I looked around behind me over my left shoulder just in time to see Mister Deputy Pig getting up off the ground, cuz he fell in the dirt when the chopper fired up, Who's laughing now, fuck face?

Answer: Me.

So Randal kicked over his Purple 73 Chopper, slapped it into gear and off into the cold darkness we rode, not having a clue where we were going. We only knew we had to get outta Dodge. This picture here is one riding down the mountain canyon road. I ain't got no midnight pictures cuz they wouldn'ta turned out anyhow.

Chapter 7:

Outa Gas

So, we got kicked outta the road side Rest Area for violating their sacred No Overnight Camping rule. The 74 Shovel Stroker was kinda cold cuz we were still up over 5,000 foot elevation and it was already after midnight. Randal and the Deputy Pig pushed started me twice, first time failed, and the second time the engine caught and fired up, with the piggy falling down in the dirt road and me laughing at him as I sat there with my bum leg on the idling chopper while Randal was kicking over his 73 Shovel. So both choppers were running and the cops were now in their squad car watching us ride away to make sure we left Dodge this time around.....and we did.

Well, there we were, riding off into the dark night without anyone around. The little 2 lane highway was totally deserted, pitch black except for our 2 headlights bouncing along on the pavement in front of us. We didn't have time to look at our map and plan a route due to our hasty departure, so we really didn't have a clue as to where we were going, we were just riding choppers down a road somewhere after midnight out in the middle of nowhere north of Antlers in northern Colorado and we were freezing our butts off.

There was only one good thing I remember about this night. The sky. I had never seen a sky so big and so dark with so many zillions of bright ass stars. It was incredible. The moon was not full, but maybe 3/4 full and was casting some light along with our headlights. Now for those of you who live or ride through the high country, you know there is one important thing you gotta be really careful of, and that one thing is, ...falling rocks. There was a sheer rock cliff on the right side of us, then on the left side, ...nothing. Another cliff off the side of the road that dropped down to the river. So we needed to be extra careful on this dark ride out in the middle of nowhere, see?

Now sometimes those falling rocks can be just little shits, like pea gravel size, and sometimes they can be as big as bowling balls, or maybe as big as your kitchen table, or maybe as big as your car or a Greyhound bus. You never know what's around the corner. The reason I am mentioning this is cuz that is why we were riding kinda slow, like around 45 mph or so.

Now we were putting along OK and then the next terrible thing happened. Randal's 73 Shovel just up and died. He was coasting along next to me for a second, then he hit the reserve quick, popped his suicide clutch out while back in gear and it fired right up,.....whew! He was just outta gas, it was not electrical problems on this hellish night please, chopper gods, We rode on for a bit and Randal's 73 was running good again, but now we know he needs gas and there sure as hell ain't no gas stations out there in the middle of nuthin', right? So I motioned for him to pull over and we did, and we shut the Shovels off. Randal was wondering what I was up to, so I told him we gotta get you some gas-mo-line. He sez how? I said like this.....

And I rummaged through the duffelbag and found a can of,....wait for it,..... Wolf Brand Chili! I had packed it all the way from Dallas. I always carried a coupla cans of chili and beans for emergency food. I dug out the mess kit and found my can opener and opened that sucker up. Now to those of you that have been reading this tripe from the beginning, you might remember that I said out of maybe 25 meals on the road for 9 days, there were 4 meals that I remembered really good. Now I never said all 4 were good meals, I just said I remember them, and this was Meal #2 which I will never forget.

We took turns eating that can of Wolf Brand,...not over a nice hot campfire, but really cold, on the side of that road and the chili musta been around 38 degrees or so,.....yummy, eh? When we got the can empty, I pulled off my fuel line and used gas to clean out the can good. Then I put a few chili cans of Ethyl into Randal's 73. I was only able to do this back then cuz I was running that big ass 4-gallon tank you can see in the pictures, so I had gas to spare. Today I run a smaller tank, so it would be bad news, hah.

Next, Randal kicked over both chops and we were off again, into the cold dark star-studded night. We rode for maybe 20 or 30 more minutes, when waaaay up ahead, we spied two bright lights shining off in the distance. The closer we got, the more we could make it out. They were not UFOs, ha-ha, but they did turn out to be two really bright lights up on top of two really tall poles, like telephone poles, but much higher. And guess what else was there? A dark and closed gas station and some dark little buildings.

When we got up to where the turn off from the highway was, we turned left and rode acrost this little bridge over the river and turned into left again into where the gas station was, and it was on the left side of the dirt road. Across the road was another building on the right side and it turned out to be a motel office, with the Vacancy and No Vacancy neon sign. There were maybe 4 or 5 little log cabins at this place, too. So, we shut off the Shovelheads and it was funny how quiet it got. Then we banged on the door and woke the poor ol' guy up and we got us one of them little motel cabins. How romantic, huh? This picture here is one Randal took of the 74 Shovel and 24-year-old me riding next to one of those rock cliff walls the next day.

Chapter 8:

UTAH DOWN TO FOUR CORNERS MONUMENT.

We woke up the next morning feeling pretty damn good from getting to sleep on a real mattress instead of the hard Colorado Rocky Mountains ground. They don't call it "Rocky" fer nuthin'.... get it, ha-ha? We even got to take hot showers and we put on clean clothes for the first time on this trip,...oooh la la. We loaded the tents and sleeping bags back onto the choppers and Randal kicked them over and we rode about 100 yards to the log cabin gas station and filled up the gas tanks and checked our oil. Then Randal kicked them over again and we rode across the dirt road to the log cabin cafe and had a nice breakfast, bacon eggs hash browns and toast, and gulped down some hot coffee to get a good start on the day. But first, we had one more really important thing to do. We moseyed over around the side of the cafe away from their windows and fired up a big fattie and got a good buzz going for the morning ride. Then Randal had to kick both choppers over again to leave for hittin' the road. See how tired poor ol' Randal's leg is getting on this trip? He's had to kick our two choppers over 6 times so far this morning and we ain't even left the log cabins yet, what a good kickin' knee, eh?

Our plan was to ride into the Utah Rockies next, then head on down through Moab and still further south to where that Four Corners Monument is, cuz we wanted to stand in 4 states at once. Why not? So I don't remember for 100% sure, but I think we got onto I-70 to ride west into Utah, simply cuz there ain't many---or any---other roads to take out there. We figured it would be most of the day's ride to get to Four Corners. And it was.

OK, now I gotta get rid of these three pictures right now. One shows the rocks that were always falling on the roads in the high country, one shows how high up we were on the choppers, and the other one shows what it looked like looking over the side of the road, where there weren't any guard rails, hit one of them rocks, chopper slides out from underneath you, and look out below!

We headed south in eastern Utah down to Four Corners Monument. That's the spot where you can stand in 4 states at once, Utah, Colorado, Arizona, and New Mexico. and who can resist that kinda historical tourist shit, right?

We got there just before dark and camped there for the night. Now those of you who have been following this drivel might recognize that this picture I am posting here does not look like the other pictures I have been posting. Why is that? Cuz all the other pictures were taken with the cheapie Kodak Instamatic, with the little round corners, but this one here ain't even a picture at all, hahaha. Nope.

It is a scan of a post card they sold at the gas station where we filled up the Shovels. I figured I'd just get the post card as a souvenir. Then all these years later I scanned it into downloads like the rest of the regular pictures to post. So now you know the story, it is not a photo I took.

Next up on the agenda, we are headed east across the top of New Mexico off to Taos, over some really winding little highways and the elevation is still well over 6,000 feet, mostly on Highway 64. That would eat up most of the day riding getting there.

Chapter 9:

Inflammable Gonads.

We arrived at the Four Corners Monument and we camped out in that area for the night. Broke camp the next morning, filled the Shovels gas tanks and our bellies, got a good buzz going, Randal kicked over both the choppers again and we took off east, headed toward Taos on Highway 64, still pretty high up in the mountains, 6,000 feet or so. Riding on Highway 64 takes you through the Navajo Nation land, some really nice desolate country, not really a place you'd wanna have a break down, though, right? So we kept puttin' on, Taos was about 5 or 6 hours away.

We were about 1/2 or maybe 2/3rds of the way to Taos when it happened. It was not raining, I was not pissing my pants, but somehow the next thing I knew my crotch was wet I looked down in time to see gas dripping out the back tab of the big black gas tank. Oh shit. And the gas that was not coming back on me was dripping down on the hot motor. Oh joy. I motioned to Randal what was going on, so we pulled over. But what are ya gonna do on the side of the road with a leaky gas tank except stare at it? Not one damn thing, that's what It was dripping maybe 2 or 3 drips every 5 seconds, so it coulda been much worse. I grabbed the two red shop rags I had with me and tried wrapping them around the backbone of the frame and the tank mounting tab to make a shield for it. Randal kicked the choppers over again and off we went.

Well as soon as the rags got wet, it was back to normal, with my crotch getting wet, ha-ha. Finally…we came upon a little town, I don't even remember the name of it, but they did have an auto parts store there. Randal was a Detroit Diesel mechanic back in Dallas and he knew his shit when it came to wrenching and the new products that were out. He told me about some stuff called JB Weld and he went in to get some while I pulled the gas tank off the 74. I leaned the tank up against a tree with the fat front side down and the leaky back end sticking up so Randal could work his JB Weld Magic. He coated it good, top and bottom. There was a cafe there so we went to eat lunch while the JB Weld started to set up. Since it was gonna take a few hours for it to cure, we decided that was as far as we were going that day.

Luckily there was also a little motel there, so we got a cheapie room. Since it wasn't running now, Randal had to push my bike over to the motel parking lot while I hobbled along on the walking cane with the now leaky swap meet gas tank, hahaha. But talk about One Stop Shopping? How lucky we found a place to get JB Weld which I had never heard of, a place to eat, and a place to crash for the night. We washed clothes and the shop rags, did some weed puffs and had our second night of non camping and ate supper in the same cafe across the street. It was our new home for maybe 12 hours or so. The next morning will be a new day.

Chapter 10:

TAOS REFILL

We left off last time with Randal teaching me all the magic wonders of this new shit called JB Weld, we had a little cheapie motel room and spent the night in the small town maybe 3 hours west of Taos still on Highway 64. Woke up the next morning and the JB Weld had set up like steel, it was awesome, I still remember how impressed I was. I put the gas tank back on the 74 Shovel, hooked up the fuel line, we ate breakfast, packed the road gear on and gassed up the choppers and got ready to hit the road.

I don't mean to whine 42 years later, but my right kicking knee was still really swollen, sore and fucked up. Back then if I had to lay the bike down for a car pulling out in front of me or some other shit like that, I preferred to lay it down on the left primary side, cuz all it would do is scratch up the Phase 3 derby cover, and once it broke a clutch hub stud, but that was it, no big deal really. However, laying it down on the right hand carb side might fuck up the exhaust pipes and the air breather, and maybe even more shit. And 2 days before we were to start this trip was when I went down in the spilt pea gravel at the end of my own damn street, and that back wheel slid out from under me so damn fast I had no idea it was gonna do it. And looking back now, when the rear slid out to the left, that made my right leg go down to brace the fall, and I musta done what they call hyperextending today. It bent over backwards the way it is not supposed to, did not break anything, but was sooo fuckin' sore I could barely walk this entire trip, even with the cane. I felt like a 60 year old grannie could kick my ass if she wanted to, hah. I suppose when I threw that right knee out,

I coulda just laid in bed with ice on it and maybe gotten better in a few days, but that ain't what happened. We had the trip planned for a long time, and Randal, being the low guy on the totem pole at his shop, had to take these days and could not change his plan. There was no choice, we had to go.

And on this trip, even with Randal being the Automatic Chopper Starter, I still had to use my right leg for the rear brake, cuz the rear brake is the only brake I had, no front brake, and I had to use my right leg to hold up the fully packed bike at red lights, cuz we both had suicide clutches. So my right knee was kinda getting worse instead of better, plus I was walking on it. The reason I am mentioning this whiny shit is cuz this morning heading out for Taos it was extra sore, ha-ha. But Randal hung in there like a champ and kept kicking it for me. I look back now and wonder what woulda happened if his knee woulda gone out?

Anyhow Randal kicked the choppers over and off to Taos we went. We got into Taos around lunch time. And to those that have been reading this old saga, you might remember me previously saying how there were 4 meals we ate on this trip that I will remember to my dying breath, and our lunch in Taos was Meal #3 for me to remember. We were out west of town and the road going in was nice, smooth and straight. When we got in Taos, we were both starving to death. And one of the first things we saw was a Mexican restaurant on the right-hand side of the road, so we pulled in to their parking lot and shut the choppers off and went in. After all, we were both raised in Dallas so Mexican food was right up our alley. We went in and the air conditioning felt good, cuz it was kinda warm that day. We ordered a big pitcher of another thing kinda new to us, Frozen Margaritas the icy slushy kind.

We started gulping down the frozen drinks and we both ordered Chicken Enchiladas, and these enchiladas came with something I had never seen before, that green Salsa Verde sauce, and damn! They were tasty. I still order the green sauce to this day.

While we were slugging back the tequila concoction, we started ratchet jawing about our road trip so far. We were laughing about the midnight ride on White Crosses and Black Beauties across the Texas Panhandle all night the first night. And we blabbed about the local Sheriff in Creede, the nice guy with the cowboy hat and boots, with the 6 point star badge and 6 shooter. And we laughed about the 2 pigs that kicked us outta camp in the middle of the night, and then even laughed about the leaky gas tank getting my gonads drenched. It was like we were remembering a trip we had taken a long time before, but we were still on it and hadn't even finished it yet. I guess that's what tequila and weed can do to you, eh? So, we filled up our bellies and gas tanks again, and got ready to head off to Tucumcari next.

Chapter 11:

SKINNY DIPPIN'.

After eating Mexican food and drinking nice frosty cold frozen margaritas for lunch. That means we had a killer buzz going and we were getting ready to ride them Shovel choppers on over to Tucumcari. So, we fired up another fatty just to make sure we had a nice buzz for the ride, cuz it was good riding weather now. We were still pretty high up in elevation, but it wasn't snowy cold or night time frigid like before, it was just nice riding weather with a jacket on.

Tucumcari was about a 4-hour ride away for us, which meant we'd get there about the end of the riding day. Rode the choppers along Highway 104, going kinda southeast. We got a camp site just outside Tucumcari, threw up the pup tents and got a little camp fire going. We had a nice little creek maybe 8 or 10 feet wide off to the side of us. For supper that night we opened 2 cans of Ranch Style Beans and put 'em in the camp fire and warmed them up good, til bubblin', then I grabbed them outta the fire with the pliers from my tool bag and we ate 'em all up.....burp.

Then we kinda started gettin' all sad like, cuz this trip is coming to an end. We're not that far from Dallas now, cuz Tucumcari sits close to the New Mexico-Texas border. That means we are gonna hafta go back to work soon,...or at least Randal is, cuz I still can't walk without a cane, so my carpenter foreman probably wouldn't like that. After bullshitting and playing poker by the camp fire for a while, we finally climbed into the tents and dozed off to the sound of the creek water going over the rocks right next to us.

I took this picture here in Tucumcari, our last New Mexico stop at a gas station.

Randal was the first one to get up in the morning and started yelling for me to get my lazy butt up, even though we were both suffering a bit of a tequila hangover, suddenly Randal shucked off his clothes down to his skivvies and jumped into the creek, then dared me to do it. So of course, I did. That's how we got 'clean' that morning, or at least it's how we started the morning, ha-ha. Breakfast was some junk outta the vending machines at the camp ground office. We didn't wanna eat much for breakfast cuz we had a special plan in store for lunch time for that day.

Anyhow we rolled up the sleeping bags and tents and loaded the gear on the choppers. Randal kicked 'em both over and down the dusty road we went. We headed east out of Tucumcari and rode on I-40 for a bit, crossed the Texas border and headed on for Amarillo, where we stopped and got gas. Now we just had a few more miles to go for our Huge Famous Lunch Spot. (Any of you reading this who live or have ridden in that area might know what I am talking about and may have already guessed it, ha-ha.)

From Amarillo, we jumped onto our old White Cross Friend Highway 287 which runs right into Carendon, Texas, about an hour or so away. Clarendon is our destination for the best eats in the universe. I took this picture out there somewhere on the dusty highway. It's getting close to lunch time and we're starving to death. Who can guess where we are headed?

Chapter 12:

MRS. BROMLEY'S DINING ROOM

Notice, this is a vintage photo.....not shot with my Kodak Instamatic. No whinin' about it now, cuz it has to go with the story, OK?

L ast time we left off breaking camp and eating vending machine junk food for breakfast, which left us starving to death riding the Shovel Choppers from Tucumcari through Amarillo and then on down Highway 287 headed to Clarendon Texas for some mouth waterin' grub both Randal and me had heard about but never had. And the place we were headed to was called Mrs. Bromley's Dining Room, at her Boarding House.

Now a bit of history for the younger set,...back in the Olden Days before all the fockin' eye sore strip malls and road side chains like Holiday Inn took over on the interstates, there were Boarding Houses all across the USA on the old highways like Mrs. Bromley's in Clarendon. What exactly is a Boarding House? It's a fun place, usually a big two Storey house, where road weary travelers can get a decent room for the night or even stay for weeks or months if they wish. At a Boarding House, there is a huge eating room down on the main floor. And in that dining room you find massive round tables and/or long bench like tables. You eat with the folks who live there or the folks who are traveling through. That means you might be eating with a local farmer and his wife who came into town, or maybe some college kids from the Clarendon College basketball team, or maybe you're eatin' with a snake eyed shifty lawyer from Chicago. Everyone is welcome,...even lawyers, That is what a Boarding House is,....or was. Those days are sadly gone now.

Back to the story, Randal and me rode the loud noisy choppers into quiet little Clarendon and we didn't hafta ask a single person for directions cuz there were signs pointing the way, plus it was right close off the Main Drag, so it was easy to find. See there? People used to actually be able to find their way around strange towns without using dumb phones and the GPS crap they rely on today. We pulled up into the parking lot in front, shut the motors off and crawled off the Shovelheads. I grabbed my walking cane outta the duffelbag and we headed into the nice big roomy house. We could already smell the delicious cookin' goin' on.

Mrs. Bromley was a really nice old lady and she had two other nice old ladies helping her out with the cooking and the serving. It was like having three Grand Mas who were glad to see you.

Mrs. Bromley told us she gets up at five o'clock to start her biscuits and rolls, she always has lots of fresh vegetables from the local farmers, and she makes the best pan fried chicken you ever tasted. They also had a pig roast and a big ham. As soon as we'd finish a plate of food, they'd tell us to go get more, cuz there's plenty. They had a buffet set up where you'd go get whatever you wanted, and then the ladies would also come by and fill up your water and sweet tea glasses and ask if everything was OK. Sometimes a lady would come by and say stuff like "Here's some fresh fried okra I just, would you boys like some?" And after stuffing ourselves, then there's more,..... cuz here came Mrs. Bromley's famous dessert,... fresh strawberry shortcake. They also had fresh baked peach cobbler which was still warm, served with vanilla ice cream. We ate it all. I ain't kidding, we ate it all.

Now in the beginning of this saga, you might remember me blabbing about the good food on the road. This meal here,......was it! Here I am, 42 years later still remembering what it was like. I think we paid around $6.50 for all you can eat. And if Randal was here right now, he'd be laughing about how much of all that great food we devoured. And the ladies kinda looked at us a little funny when we walked in, like we might rob the place, but by the time we left, I was in love with all three of them, hahaha. And Randal was, too.

OK, now we are so fat and full, it's purdy hard to walk, much less lift up a leg over the seat to get on the bikes. And Randal has to kick start both Shovels so we can head on down the highway! Bwahahaha, poor Randal.

Chapter 13:

Road Outhouse Heaven

OK Randal and me stuffed our guts at Mrs. Bromley's Dining Room in Clarendon Texas, up by the Panhandle on Highway 287. Now it's time to head out,.....burp.

I still remember how Randal groaned as he lifted his leg to kick over my 74 AMF, ha-ha, it sputtered and fired, I crawled on it, then he had to go kick start his Purple 73 Shovelhead. Now both chops are running, we had filled 'em with Ethyl, and then we took on off down the dusty trail known as Highway 287 headed toward Fort Worth & Dallas. We were looking at about a 6 hour ride. It's around 300 miles from Clarendon to Dallas, but remember the speed limit in 1979 was still 55 mph back then, and we didn't need to get pulled over by The Man for speeding, right? Right. The object is to complete the trip with as few encounters with The Law as possible. And we'd already had a bad one in Colorado, hah.

So we rode and bounced on along on the two rigid choppers with overfilled bellies, and next thing ya know, something kinda nasty was about to happen. Now for those of you who are squeamish or could be eating or drinking something right now, you might wanna skip the next paragraph, cuz it gets kinda nasty. Remember, you have been warned.

(OK if you are still reading this one, get ready for some nastiness. In my effort to give you all the nitty gritty details of this 1979 road trip, I have been as honest and upfront as possible telling you what happened all along the way. Therefore, I will not shy away from this next sordid affair

. What happens when you eat too much? What happens when you eat too much and you are out in the middle of nowhere bouncing along the highway on a rigid framed chopper? Next thing ya know, I had a really uncomfortable feeling, like I was getting ready to explode. But I didn't wanna complain and seem like a wimp to Randal who was riding over next to me in the other side of our lane, so I didn't say nuthin'.

We hit a few more bumps in the road. It got worse. Both sets of Shovel exhaust pipes were rumbling, but not as much as my belly was. I felt like I was gonna blow up. Then suddenly Randal looked over at me in extreme pain and then he yells out over our exhaust pipe racket,....."I GOTTA TAKE A SHIT!" LOL And so did I, so we started yelling back and forth about what we were gonna do. I mean, it got sooo bad if we didn't find a gas station, cafe, motel, hardware store, a tumbleweed, ANYTHING to pull over to, we were gonna be in deep shit,...literally. Finally, we saw a road sign saying there was a Rest Area coming up 4 miles away, so we twisted the throttles and made a mad dash for relief. Then I started to panic. What if there is only one toilet? Randal will surely beat me to it cuz I'm on a walking cane. What if somebody is already in the bathroom, and neither one of us can go in,...what then? But the Chopper Gods musta been smiling on us that day, cuz the Rest Area came up and there were over a half dozen stalls in the men's room and they were all empty, yay! And that is the highlight of our road trip for that day, Mrs. Bromley's Dining Room and that Rest Area, where we blew the bottoms outta those toilets....

***OK, now back to the rest of the normal story for the squeamish folks. We rode on into the Texas sunset and early evening, ridin' along with the 18 wheelers just as we had when we left Texas going the other way a few days earlier, and we were stopping only for gas and to stretch our legs and to do a puff or two,...or three. We didn't need to eat anymore, LOL. We finally got into the Fort Worth traffic and things were starting to remind us this road trip was now over. And then?

Then we saw the sign that said Randal's exit was coming up ahead. We looked at each other ridin' in the wind for one last time, did palm slaps to say farewell, and then,..... that was it. Randal peeled off on the right-hand exit ramp headed to his place, which left me riding all alone now, just one set of pipes making their noise. It felt really weird going on alone. Maybe I needed some modern day therapy for suffering this separation, It was strange, been with the guy for 8 days, every waking moment, listening to our two Shovels having their say, from listening to their exhaust pipes bouncing off the canyon walls in Colorado to hearin' 'em blastin' as we were roaming across the New Mexico and Texas flat land desert, to now this,.....nuthin'. The road trip is over.

And then the second thought hit me. "I AIN'T GOT RANDAL NO MORE!" What if my 74 Shovel burps and dies at a red light? Who's gonna kick it for me, Bahahaha? Anyhow, we made it back home. These pictures are out on the Highway and back home with my 74 AMF Chopper. Sadly, I never got any more pictures of Randal's Purple 73 Shovel, and neither did he.

And once we were back home in Dallas, about a week later we tore both Shovels down for total rebuilds, from sandblasted frames back up. I got mine done, including a new motor and tranny build by Joe Cox, in a grand total of 5 weeks and 6 days. Here's the last photos of the 74 AMF in its 1979 Road Trip stage.

Chapter 14:

THE BLACK IMRON PAINT

A fter the Randal Kick Start Trip from the summer of 1979, my knee eventually got better,...I think,...and we rode our choppers around Dallas and Fort Worth, had fun drinking and shooting pool, chasin' tail, you know the drill. Then came late fall rains, and Randal and me both tore our Shovel choppers down to bare sand-blasted frames. Randal got to set his motor and tranny aside cuz they had a recent build from the previous owner. But my 74 AMF needed a new build, it was gettin' kinda ticky, knocky, and smokin' a wee bit.

My local Chopper Guru Shelby Withrow of Mid Cities Choppers was busy up to his neck in work. But I was lucky to get an ace Harley mechanic in Arlington named Joe Cox to do my motor and tranny.

So while Joe was busy doing the engine and 4 speed, I set in on the frame. This was gonna be my best build yet. Although I was only a 24 year old punk kid, I had already done 5 bare frame up builds on the 74, the Twisted Springer build, the Flame Cut Girder build, the 15 over Swap Meet Leaky Wide Glide build, the cut frame Barney Sliders build, and the 1979 Randal Trip Wide Glide build.

This frame here is the basis of the next build. It was an old 1971 D&D Jammer frame I got used from one of the Scorpions in Dallas.

He wanted a swing arm, I wanted a rigid, so Shelby stepped in and helped arrange the swap. To those that have been following its story, in 1978 I took a hack saw and cut the neck off this frame, at the seat post and foot pegs area. And Dangerous George and the old Southern California ex Galloping Goose Dutch in Arlington welded up the new neck for me.

This picture here is in my own little house's front yard. Randal had his Purple 73 Shovel torn apart over at his place. But his progress wasn't as fast as mine was. When I offered to help him out, he kinda gave me the ol' brush off, And I don't blame him. He was a good mechanic by trade, so why would he want some ol' sawdust eatin' carpenter telling him what to do?

Randal was lucky cuz his motor and tranny had just been gone through by the guy he got it from. Mine was another story. Aside from the Randal Road Trip, it had been on a few others, Daytona, Sturgis, Calgary Alberta, up the dirt road to the top of Pikes Peak, plus back then I rode it to work and everywhere else. To those of you who have kinda lived on your bike, you know what I mean.

So once I got down to bare sandblasted frame, I started in on the molding job. This was gonna be my finest build yet,...hopefully,...if I didn't screw it up, hah. I had been impressed by the choppers I saw in Easyriders, Choppers, and Street Choppers magazines. I wanted something along those lines, pretty well detailed. I had never molded a frame before but I had seen the articles in the mags, so I set in with mixing the ol' Bondo.

I worked on that frame every night after work with my bloody fingers until I got it bee-yoo-tee-full, in Bondo. Then I primed it myself. Then the guys I ran with had a painter in our mix. His name was Terry and he worked over in Arlington at Good Times Vans, where they did custom mural paint work on vans. Terry was also a Shovelhead chopper guy, but his was apart at this time. He was married and had 4 kids, he needed some bucks to get his bike going, so I paid him some cash money to spray the 74 AMFer. Terry used a new-fangled paint he told me about, called Imron, and it was a very tough paint they were using for semi-trucks front ends, cuz it was rock chip and bug resistant. So, I said sure why not? Go for it.

So early one December Saturday morning I hung up the frame, tank, and back fender by coat hangers from the rafters in my little 1 car garage. Terry came over with his spray rig and started in. Man, I tell ya, the black fog was THICK shit, and we were laughing and getting high off the fumes. Later we found out it is a toxic paint and will eat your brain cells, so maybe that's what's wrong with me today. After Terry finished spraying, we set out on my front porch and smoked a joint and had a coupla beers. Then Terry said "Let's go see how it turned out." When we walked into the garage, I was blown away by how wonderful that paint job was. The painted parts looked like they were made out of black glass. The gas tank looked like I could take my finger and thump it and it would shatter like a Christmas ornament.

Meanwhile Joe Cox was busy with the motor and tranny. I went in to work on the wide glide and front wheel with no brake. I was gonna run the same chrome fender I had gotten at Brown's Custom Cycles on Main Street in downtown Dallas a coupla years before,...for $19.95, plus tax. So I got busy and got the chassis done about the time Joe finished the motor and tranny builds, and I put those in the chassis, wired the focker up and had a running bike again. Total time for the new build? 5 weeks and 6 days. Not too shabby for a punk kid, eh?

Meanwhile, Randal still has his 73 Shovel Chopper stripped down and is gonna paint it gold. This here is a picture of my new build for late December, 1979, and the picture is taken on top of Cedar Hill, Texas.

Here's another shot of the new build on the 74 AMF Chopper. And to those of you that have been following this sordid story, you might notice that leaky sumbitch gas tank with the hidden spine gas cap that nearly set my nuts on fire in New Mexico is now,.....GONE!

That's right. No more cheap leaky ass swap meet used gas tanks for me, bwah ha-ha. This tank here is one I got brand new from Shelby's Mid Cities Choppers shop. It is a Paughco Mustang tank, holds 3.2 gallons, and is the one I still run today, 42 years later. Got my money's worth on that one, huh? I also put that Tank Seal shit in it, so even if a weld ever does let go, it ain't gonna leak on my you-know-whatses.

As for Randal's build on his 73 Shovel Chopper? You probably ain't gonna like this part of the story and I sure didn't either. He got it painted a really nice metallic gold, put the motor and tranny in, wired it up, got it running, and then some guy with a 1977 Tan Corvette said he wanted Randal's chopper, offered to trade, and Randal did the swap. I cried and cried, "Don't do it. Don't do it." But he did it. This was 1979 and I guess a really nice 2 year old Corvette was what Randal wanted. Maybe it rode a little bit easier than the rigid?

This photo here is at a real old timey boneyard, graves from the 1800s, on top of Cedar Hill, Texas, 1979.

Chapter 15:

KRAZY SOLO ROAD TRIP

February 1980, I turned 25 and the 74 AMF Chopper was on its 6th new bare frame up build, my best build yet. In other words, it was not a black rattle can spray bomb like the previous 5 builds were, I built this version in the living room of my house. And now with the new Joe Cox motor and tranny build, and the molded frame with the slick Black Imron paint job sprayed by my good buddy Terry, it was fit for the road trip to top all my previous road trips.

I was getting ready to leave Dallas for good. No offense to you Texas friends, but I cannot take that summer heat, hah. I am a carpenter and working in 104 or 108 degrees is not my idea of having fun. So I made The Plan to Leave. How did I make the plan? Kinda in a goofy way. I got out my big road atlas map book of the USA and looked for a state far away that had mountains, rivers, lakes, an ocean would be nice, a bunch of trees, and not that many people.

I looked at Maine and Vermont. But in order to get there, I'd hafta ride through and deal with millions of people in the New England area. (No offense to you in the New England area, hah.) Then I looked straight up north by Montana, but although they had mountains, they didn't look like they had towns big enough to keep a strange new carpenter in town busy enough to eat and pay the bills, hah. Then I looked over to the Pacific Northwest and thought of Washington State. I didn't know a soul there. But at a previous family Christmas get together in Dallas, a cuzzin of mine who had lived up in Anchorage told me about a town he went through called Ellensburg, in Washington. He said it was mostly a farm town, population around 10,000 people back then, and said it sat right in the valley with rivers mountains on both sides, plus it was also a college town for some fun, with the Central Washington University there. And then there was the Pacific Ocean over on the side. OK. It's Washington. Why not?

I decided to leave everything I had ever known that was familiar and roll the dice to find something new. Maybe I'd have some fun, maybe I'd fall flat on my face. And I'd be riding off alone this time. Seems all my Texas riding partners were no more. Randal had just traded his 73 Shovel Chopper for a 1977 Corvette. My younger brudder got T-Boned at an intersection by a dumb ass in a car running a red light. The accident broke his 71 Shovel Chopper in half. His Durfee girder got busted off the front end, snapped the fork stem off. That left him the back end of his chopper, motor and tranny sitting in the frame with the back wheel still on there. Some low life mutha fockin' thief stole the back end of my brudder's 71 Shovel out of his back yard, and it had been under a tarp with a fence and dog. Anyhow, they got it, but they left the Durfee layin' there on the ground cuz they could see it was busted. (By the way, that is the same Durfee girder on the 74 AMF Chopper today.)

My buddy Gary had sold his 75 Sportster, Ray got rid of his 72 Shovel, Kim had his 76 Shovel stolen, Terry's Shovel was still in pieces, he never got it running. Mike sold his white Shovelhead.

And the older guys I had ridden with a few years before, Shelby, Harold and Blue Jay now had wives and kids they were taking care of. So, what had been a mid-1970s fun filled life with tons of bikes at my house all the time and lots of friends to ride with was now kinda gone.

Hank Jr. "But nobody wants to get high on the town, and all my rowdy friends have settled down."

So I made the fateful decision against everybody's advice, and put my little house up for sale. In 1973 when I was 18 working lots of OT building the Braniff Terminal at the DFW Airport, I got the house for $12,500, my payments were 104 a month, imagine that today? After being in it for 7 years, the price I got for it was $25,000, so it exactly doubled. I paid off what was left on the mortgage, paid off some other bills, put my carpenter tools, Technics stereo and all my many record albums, 19 inch Color TV,...ooh la la,... and boxes of motorsickle parts in a storage unit and paid them up for 3 months in advance, which would give me plenty of time to figure out what I was gonna do. Furniture and other stuff I gave away to whoever wanted it. These are the last pictures of the 74 AMF Chopper living in Dallas, early 1980.

Chapter 16:

LEAVING DALLAS

L eft off last time selling the shacky little house in Dallas, putting a few things in storage and getting ready to hit the road on the 74 AMF Chopper. In preparation for the big road trip, the build is now brand new again, motor and tranny by Joe Cox in Arlington Texas, new tires, chain, brake shoes on the mechanical brake on back,..... still no front brake. lol,.....new gas tank, and on this 6th build I finally honed the art of getting the back wheel, fender, oil tank, frame and fender to fit nice and tight like one unit with no space showing in between like my previous builds had,...amateur shit. This is also the new Drag Specialties oil tank cuz the drunk American Airline's pilot caved in my original Harley oil tank out by DFW when he T Boned me in the middle of the highway coming up from the median, yes I will tell that sordid tale and others in another book sometime.

So, at this stage the new motor has 4- & 1/2-inch stroker S&S flywheels, is bored .40 over, got a big honkin' 44 mm Mikuni carb, suicide clutch and stick shift, full set of Andrews gears in the tranny with a Barnett clutch and a big ol' 25 tooth countershaft sprocket geared for top end and easy cruisin' to go loping down the highway.

As for packing up the road gear,...we got the precious tool bag. a duffelbag that's got some jeans, long johns, heavy gloves in case it gets cold,...and it did,...some socks and skivvies. I never bothered to pack t shirts cuz I'd get them out on the road at various shops for souvenirs,...why not? All this is gonna go on back with bungie cords, and we gotta have the tent and sleeping bag, and something special that's gonna go inside the headlight,

And that something special is an ounce of Hawaiian weed, the kind with the purple hairs that cost 50 bucks for the lid. Oh my. That was some expensive shit, lol. And since I had a little over 10 grand from the house sale, there is a cashier's check made out to myself for 10 grand, the most money I ever had in my life, even more than I've got today, I gently rolled up that cashier's check like a joint in a baggie to keep it waterproof and then I wrapped it up like a burrito in aluminum foil in case I had to use the head light and it got hot inside the light shell. Do not wanna burn up 10 grand...right? It would take me years to get that much loot again.

And all the weed got wrapped in aluminum foil and stuck inside the back of the head light except for 3 joints that I stuck inside the left handlebar grip. There. Now everything is hidden and the cops can pull me over and frisk me and they won't find jack shit.

It's gonna be a full day's ride to get to the New Mexico border up by Raton, going up the ol' trusty Highway 287 again, acrost the Texas Panhandle. My brudder Chuck was there in the yard when I left and so was our buddy Vance who I had known since junior high school 1967, and back then he worked at a store called Best Products, kinda like a Best Buy today. Vance was a camera genius and he hooked me up with a Canon AE-1 35 mm camera from Best Produxts. And that's good for you guys, cuz that means from now on the pictures will be 35 mm ones now instead of the cheapie little blurry Kodak Instamatics, this is the last picture of the 74 AMF Chopper in Texas before we throw the tent and sleeping bag on and take off for parts unknown. It's time to kick it over now and point the front wheel to the north west.

This was gonna be my first One Way Road Trip where I wasn't coming back for a while. And it was also gonna be the first road trip for this new build, and I was hoping like hell it would all hang together, Cuz when a 24 year old kid builds a chopper in his living room, who knows what shit will fall off, right? Just kidding, the bike performed just fine.

When I was leaving the Fort Worth area headed onto Highway 287, I had two feelings fighting each other in my belly. And no, it wasn't poop related this time part of me was very excited about taking off on a trip where I had no idea what lay ahead, while the other part of me was asking 'what the fuck are you doing?' I was leaving everything I had ever known, which I will admit was scary as hell. No more family or friends to rely on if things went bad, no steady job, no familiar riding buddies, no familiar bars or pool halls, no nuthin'.

It was around 500 or so miles to the New Mexico border from Dallas. And since I left kinda in the afternoon, I camped along the way, maybe 300 miles out. Well, I didn't really 'camp' I just threw the sleeping bag on top of a picnic table along the way at one of those Road Side Rest Areas,...the kind where ya ain't supposed to do overnight camping, As you can tell by the shadow on the ground in this picture at the New Mexico border, it was maybe around 2 or 3 in the afternoon when I got to the border the next day. It's over 2,000 miles from Dallas to Washington State where I was headed, and that was about the same distance as the time I rode from Dallas to Calgary, and we are talking Sore Butt Category on the second day, I still ain't never figured out why my butt got sore on the second day, first day was fine, third, fourth, fifth days were fine, but that second day always got me good.

Chapter 17:

New Mexico to Colorado

This is another desolate shot riding through New Mexico. I got off to stretch my legs, take another big ol' puff of Hawaiian devil weed, and ask myself if I was really doing the right thing, leaving everyone and everything I knew behind? It's times like this that building up a trusty chopper you can depend on pays off. No smart phones, no GPS, no Emergency Road Service, nobody else I was riding with,... just the 74 AMF Chopper, the wide open road, and 25 year old me,...out in the middle of nowhere.

Here, out in the middle of nowhere in New Mexico, up in the northeast corner of the state. Rode on up Highway 64 and there's the Colorado border coming up next.

So we crossed over the Colorado border, I was ridin' up the eastern side of the state this time, not over into the beautiful western Rockies like we did on the Randal Trip a few months earlier. Around the Trinidad area Highway 160 joins up with I-25 headed north, on up toward Pueblo.

It is still kinda desolate country, but cruising' on the Interstate now made for better time. So far the weather had been just fine, but a trucker in a road side truck stop cafe warned me about some heavy rains up ahead. This is still out there in southeastern Colorado.

Ridin' up I-25 now, I stopped at a truck stop along the way, I was getting gas and stuffin' my face when a trucker sitting at the counter told me of some massive rain up ahead. I told him I'm from Texas and we're used to massive downpours, but that don't mean I like ridin' in 'em. So I stopped in at a camp ground south of Pueblo for the night and set up the tent. Pueblo is about a 2 hour ride south of Denver, so that gave me about 600 miles on the trip so far. This is the last picture I took befoe the big rain storm, and no, I did not get any pictures of the monsoon cuz I didn't wanna get the new Canon AE-1 wet, That thing cost a few bucks, it wasn't no 15 dollar Kodak Instamatic. And here's a weird thing about this picture, the 74 AMF Chopper is facing the wrong way over on the shoulder, I musta turned it around to show the carb side for a change, and you can see the big clouds forming in the distance.

Chapter 18:

WET IN THE MIDDLE OF NOWHERE

Last chapter we left off setting up the tent at a for real campground south of Pueblo, Colorado, the kind where you pay some money for your designated site and the cops can't run you off for overnight camping, ha-ha. The trucker at the last truck stop had warned me about a huge rainstorm that was coming our way, and he was right sadly. The first drops started falling about the time I finished setting up the tent. Back then I always carried plastic bags with me for times such as this. I took a plastic bag and wrapped it around the 44 mm MIkuni to try to keep it dry inside and wrapped a big rubber band around it in case it got windy. By 1980 I had experience with only three different kinds of carbs, the Tillotson on the 67 Sportster, the stock Bendix that came on the 74 AMF Shovelhead when it was brand new, and the 44 mm Mikuni that I got from Shelby when he first stroked the motor in September 1975.

I loved that Mikuni, even though the guys on the old Harley choppers would give me shit about putting a Japanese carb on my Shovelhead. But then I'd remind them how they always told me it's just a fuckin' bowling ball motor anyhow, so what does it matter to them, hah? Then if they continued, I'd politely ask 'em if they wanted to race for a beer. I don't remember ever getting any takers, for some reason. After all, who wants to put their 61 inch or 74 inch Knuckle or Pan up against a fresh 86 inch Shovel? That was kinda evil of me, huh?

Anyhow, sorry I rambled, back to the plastic bag on the Mikuni. That Mikuni was a great carb, it kick started really good and had good throttle response. But it had one big weakness. Rain. If rain got into the air cleaner, you were fucked. The slide would stick in whichever position it was in. You could twist or untwist the throttle, but it didn't do any good. You were still running at whatever rpm it was in when the round slide got wet and stuck. But after a while, I did figure out an easy fix for it. What displaces water?

WD-40 to the rescue, that's right, WD-40 got rid of the water and my problem would be solved,.....until the next time it got stuck in the rain, which could be next week or in an hour. For preventive care, I'd stick the plastic bag on if it was parked, and if I was riding in a rain storm, I'd loop my right knee around the front of the air cleaner to keep some of the rain out. It kinda helped some. But what else could I do?

So I went to sleep the best I could that night in the tent with the rain pouring down. Next morning, I woke up and it was still raining. Oh great. Just what I needed,... a nice soaking wet ride to start the day. I rolled up the sleeping bag trying to keep it as dry as I could, then rolled up the soaking wet tent. Packed them on the chopper with rain still coming down, took off the plastic bag on the Mikuni, kicked it over and started out to the highway headed north.

I pulled into the first place I came to that had gas and food. Ate and filled up the gas tank and it was still pouring rain. I started riding north again going up I-25 headed toward Denver, the Mile High City. As I was riding along in the rain, I remembered one of my dad's sayings about big rain storms, and his saying fit this rain perfectly. "It was raining drops as big as horse turds." And it was, But hey, you can only get so wet, right? I mean, once the rain has soaked your jacket and gloves, and once you have the rain running down your back to your butt crack, and once you have the rain running down in your crotch, and once you have your feet all squishy wet in your boots, you ain't gonna get much wetter, so ya might as well push on, and push on I did.

Just before I got into Denver, I was up on top of a hill looking down into a valley, torrential buckets of rain still falling. This rain shit was not letting up. I looked down the straight highway laid out in front of me. There wasn't much else around, except for a big ol' tree on the right hand side of the road. And underneath that tree was a little dot, and the closer I got, the bigger the dot got, and then it became clear to me that it was another motorcycle under the tree, and then when I got even closer, I discovered it was another chopper! I could tell it was chopped by the way it sat with the primary hanging off the left side. It was packed for the road.

(This picture here is actually after the rain, cuz like I said before, I didn't take any pictures of the rain cuz I didn't wanna get the new camera wet. So who is on that chopper parked under the tree and what the hell are they doing out here in the middle of nowhere?)

Chapter 19:

MEETING THE MYSTERY BIKER

I couldn't exactly figure out what the chopper was doing there, but two things popped into my mind. Either the guy was broke down, or else he just stopped to admire the monsoon we were trapped in, And that big tree he was parked under still didn't have any leaves on it yet, cuz it was early spring, so I didn't think he was under there for shelter.

Riding up closer to him maybe 75 yards away now, I pushed in the foot clutch and dropped the tranny back into 3rd gear, let the clutch back out and the upsweep fishtails rumbled like a jake brake on a semi. Then clicked down into 2nd, then came up to the shoulder in the rain. As I pulled up behind the chopper, the first things I noticed was it was packed for the road and had a license tag down on the lower right side by the axle and that license tag said California and it was the old black and gold one. I knew right away I was about to be in the presence of something real. I pulled on up beside the chopper on the right-hand side and its pilot was standing in front watching me ride in. I put it in neutral, flipped the toggle switch and it was shut off. All was quiet now except for the rain coming down.

I threw my right leg over the saddle, stood up and this is what I saw: An old Panhead chopper sitting in a rigid Harley frame with Shovel heads on it, well-worn shotgun pipes, a gas tank mounted high Frisco style, an early style kicker arm, mechanical brakes, and a wide glide front end with pull back bars. This old chopper was a true veteran of the road. So was its rider. He appeared to be maybe 10 years or so older than my 25 years. I suddenly felt like an apprentice chopper rider again, on my Newer Bowling Ball Motor with cut up aftermarket frame, hahaha.

I looked at the guy and said "Hi, I'm Dave." He said his name was Steve Kelly. When I asked him if he was having a problem, he said the water had finally gotten to his bike, both carb and points. I looked at his carb, it was an SU. And his points were not protected inside a cone like mine were, they were out in his circuit breaker getting wet. I told him I had one of those little spray bottles of WD-40 that I used on my water-logged carb and told him it worked for me. I was just suggesting now, mind you, cuz there was no way I was about to tell this road veteran what to do with his own chopper,...right? But he grinned and said "Let's give it a try."

So he pulled off the top screw cover on the SU's dome and I gave him the can and he shot some WD down inside the SU. Then he pulled off his breather and shot some inside, then did the same with his points and condenser. I had a semi dry red shop rag in my tool bag and was using it as a shield to keep off the rain and to wipe off the excess WD-40. Steve put the circuit breaker cover back on and tightened up the SU's top screw. Then he turned the key on, gave it a few kicks and it fired right up. He got a big grin going and so did I, and he was letting it run for a while to clean itself out. And that is when I made another suggestion..."Hey Steve, I've got a nice big fat joint of Kona bud with the little purple hairs. You want some?" He sez, "How can you possibly still have anything dry on you?",...cuz we were both still dripping in the rain, hahaha. So I said "Like this" and pulled the chrome cap off the left handlebar grip and there was the Big Fattie, all nice and dry ready to light up. So we did.

After I mentioned how I liked his old black and gold California tag, he asked me where I was from. I told him I lived in Dallas, until three days ago, now I live on this chopper seat right here. He asked me where I was headed, I said up to Washington State. He said he was headed to Coeur d'Alene Idaho and then he said we might as well ride on together, so now I had a kool new riding partner outta the blue, or right outta the rain, I should say.

So we rode on together up I-25 North until we got into Casper Wyoming. It was probably about 300 miles or so, but we stopped cuz we were dead beat. We decided no more fucking camping out that night, we got a nice big roomy motel room and there was a pizza joint and a likker store right next to it. What more could ya ask for? Hot showers and food and beer, yay!

This is the only photo I have of Steve Kelly's Panhead chopper, and this was from the next morning at the motel when it finally stopped raining.

Chapter 20:

RIDING WITH STEVE KELLY.

After crashin' at a road side motel in Casper Wyoming, I now had a brand new California riding partner on a Pan/Shovel Chopper named Steve Kelly. Anybody out there remember that name or his chopper?

Since I was still kinda loaded with cash, I sprung for a nice big roomy motel room. It was a huge ass room, two big double beds, kitchen area, nice roomy shower, and double closets with Color TV. Once we got situated in the room, we spread out all our road gear on different ends of the room. I actually set up my tent in the room to dry out. Back then it was one of those little orange nylon pup tents, if you remember those things. Of course, there was no way I could stake it to the floor, ha ha-ha, but I did put on the tent poles to stand the tent up and I tied one line to the closet door and the other line to a chair, so it was set up and could dry out pretty quick. We had all our wet clothes spread out to dry.

Now it was time for hot showers, put on some wet and cold clothes cuz nuthin' was dry yet, and then,.....hot fresh Pizza & Beer, yay! Oh,...and more Kona Bud with the purple hairs. Steve told me he was from San Francisco and he had been out on the road since January, that made me the lightweight on the road for only 3 days. He said he knew folks up in Coeur d'Alene and that's where he was headed. I said I didn't know anybody in Washington State just yet but that's where I was headed,... for a new start.

We woke up kinda early the next morning and it was nice and sunny for a change. Had breakfast at the motel cafe, filled up the gas tanks, kicked the Shovel

Chops over and took off. I was still 1,000 miles out from where I was headed, so that meant two more days on the road for me. Looking at the soggy road map, Steve still had about 800 miles to go himself. We took off, rode on up I-25 into Montana, Big Sky Country. Then around Billings we peeled off onto I-90 headed west and rode that nice big freeway through mountains. We stopped only for gas and food and to toke, then crashed for the night at a campground by Butte, Montana. That gave us around 500 miles that day, which was pretty good. And now we were back up in the high country, elevation around 5,500 feet, way up high in the mountains.

This photo here is up high in the mountains and is getting ready to pack up the camping gear again and take off.

California Steve and me had stopped the Shovelhead Choppers at a camp- ground around Butte Montana for the night. After we got the tents set up, we got a nice little fire going for some warmth. Looking at the semi-dried out road map, it looked like Steve had about 275 miles to go to Coeur d'Alene Idaho while I had about 475 miles or so to make it to Ellensburg Washington. We both decided we'd go for the gusto the next day, cuz it was supposed to be nice weather, so we might as well make hay while the sun shines...right? Besides, who wants to get caught out in another monsoon storm?

I-90 was our only highway we needed now, so we ain't got no more use for the still damp maps. All we had to do was point the front wheels west and roll on the throttles, hah. And that's what we did. We had fun riding in the good weather through the high country, or at least I know I did. It was a fun ride leaning in and out of the big turns, mountains all around us, river running next to the freeway every once in a while. We even saw eagles flying overhead.

Montana is a long ole' state when yer riding east to west, and it seemed like to me it was taking forever to cross it. Missoula finally came and then went behind us, then we were getting closer to the Idaho border and then Coeur d'Alene.

I will admit it was a kinda sad feeling when we got to Steve's exit ramp for Coeur d'Alene, and he waved me on by with his raised clenched fist and he took off down his exit ramp never to be seen by me again. It reminded me of the 1979 Randal Road Trip where Randal peeled off for his exit. Ya get kinda used to riding with somebody for a few states, having them be there, hearing their exhaust pipes blastin', and then suddenly..... they are gone, and then it's just back to only you and your bike and your bike's pipes, going down the highway by yourself again.

Oh well, I started out this long road trip by myself so it's only fitting I ended it by myself. I was lucky to have Steve through Colorado, Wyoming, Montana, and into Idaho. Funny how I accidentally ran into a guy in the middle of a downpour whose chopper was flooded out under a big tree in Colorado, and now 41 years alter that, I still remember his cool California chopper and him, and I even got a picture of his bike to remember that soggy meeting by.

I continued the ride alone now, through Spokane on I-90 and then on into Central Washington. I rode through little towns like Ritzville and Moses Lake, towns on I-90 that I would soon become very familiar with. The Shovelhead's upsweep fishtails kept rumbling through a little town called George.....George Washington,..... get it, And then I crossed the big ass Columbia River by a town called Vantage, and kept on rolling over the pass into Ellensburg, the destination. I was dead beat. I got a motel room at the Thunderbird Motel on the east end of town. I dumped off all the camping gear in the room and rode around on a bare chopper for a while, I checked out the bars downtown on their old-fashioned town square, what a natural slice of Americana. Then I rode on over to the Main Drag to a place called The Hi-way Grill, which would soon become one of my favorite places to eat, cuz not only did they have good eats, they were also open after bar time, hahaha. And the chopper felt a lot better riding it with nothing on it except my butt. Oh well. At least I had made it.

This picture here is out in the woods by Ellensburg Washington looking through some pine needles at the trusty Shovel chopper who got me all the way here, 2,000 miles. Tomorrow I gotta find a new dump to crash in for a while and check out my new home town.

Chapter 21:

BIKER BANKING

Last time the 74 Chopper had just ridden into Ellensburg Washington on I-90 from Idaho. I got a room at The Thunderbird Motel out on the east end of town. The next morning, I ate breakfast up the road from the motel at "The Hi-way Grille," a really cool old joint built in the 1940s, which became sort of a hangout for my eats plus it was close by. Next, I set about finding a dump to rent so I'd actually have a place to live cuz that Thunderbird Motel ain't exactly cheap, hah. The rent prices kinda floored me. I had my own shacky house in Dallas and the payments were 104 a month. The places I was looking to rent were 250 to 300,.....yikes!

I finally found a crash pad for 200 a month on Water Street, downtown one block off the Main Drag, and it was furnished, which was kinda cool since I didn't have any furniture, hahaha. Gave the guy first & last month's rent and there I was, an official Ellensburg resident,...sorta. And the place I rented was a duplex with a college kid in the other half, and we were right close to the Hi-way Grille and the University, with a nice burger joint right acrost the street and even a head shop a coupla blocks away. Things were starting to look up.

Next on the agenda was to get rid of that Dallas First National Bank Cashier's Check for 10 grand, which had been the money from selling the shack in Dallas. Since I was now living right downtown by the Town Square, I moseyed into the biggest old bank in town to open a savings account with the cashier's check. I would like to state for the record that I had every intention of getting a job in this town and buying a house there, but sometimes intentions and plans don't work out so hot, do they, hah?

Anyway, I walked up to the counter and I told the girl teller I'd like to open a savings account. She looked at me, sorta in disgust, I guess I'd say. I mean, it wasn't her fault, I was kinda scumbag looking, shaggy hair and beard, road worn jeans and scruffy black leather jacket, what was she supposed to think? That I was there to rob the joint, hah?

She looked at me and I will never forget what she said next. "You need to have at least 50 dollars to open a savings account here." So I opened my eyes really wide sez to her kinda loud-ish in mock disbelief, "Fifty whole dollars?" I pulled out my wallet and handed her the sorta worn and rolled up cashier's check for 10 grand and said "Will this be enough?" She didn't say nuthin'! She looked at it in her hands for a coupla seconds, then walked over to the big boss man and handed it to him with one hand and pointed at me with her other hand, Anyhow, I finally got my savings account going and I gave them the address of the dump on Water Street, and next I got a phone hooked up, the type of phone with a dial on it that most folks today wouldn't know how to use.

Now I am semi-established in Ellensburg. Next I went to the nearby lumber yard and got a nice 10 foot long 2 X 12, walked back to the dump with it, and that became my nice new ramp for the chopper to get to its nice parking spot,...inside the dump, hahaha. Hell, I ain't leaving that nice fucker outside in a strange town,.. would you? So next I hopped on a classy Greyhound Bus and took it to Seattle where I hopped a plane back to Dallas, and this was the first time for me to fly on a big jet plane. It did not crash, so that was good.

Then I went to my folks' house where I had my car stashed, the White 75 Vette that some of you saw in the Randal's Blazer picture with my bare chopper frame sitting next to it in the yard. I took the Vette to my buddy Hal's garage and we put it up on the lift, changed all fluids for the trip up to Washington, then stuck a trailer hitch on back, complete with tail light hook ups,...oooh la la.

I loaded up a litte U Haul trailer with my carpenter tool box, extra chopper parts, the busted 1976 Durfee Girder, the stereo and albums, 19 inch TV, kitchen stuff like pots and pans and the rest of my clothes and off I went, back up to Washington.

This time, I took Highway 287 as far as Amarillo, then I took Route 66 West to Los Angeles, cuz I had seen enough of Colorado Rocky Mountains from the last 6 chopper road trips going through there since 1973, hahaha. Once I hit LA and the Pacific Ocean, I simply turned right and took Highway 1 and 101 all the way up north, as far as it went. What a trip. I know this was a car trip instead of a bike trip, but that's the way it had to be, no choice. Besides, I would later make that Highway 1 and 101 trip quite a few times on the 74 AMF Chopper in the coming years. (Yes, of course there's pictures, wink, wink.)

I cruised north along the California Coast, mountains on my right, ocean on my left, watching the sun set over the Pacific Ocean. That was cool, had never seen that before. I drove across that Big Sur Bridge that Bronson rode his Sportster over, and I drove across the Golden Gate Bridge and the rest of Northern California Coast. Then I headed up the Oregon Coast, holy shit, how beautiful. I ate tons of clam chowder at the grottos along the way, had fresh red snapper and other fried fishes along the way.

When you get going good into the Washington Coast, Highway 1 North suddenly becomes Highway 1 South, cuz you go all the way around the Olympic Peninsula, until you actually go south into Seattle. It was raining in this area,...big surprise,...and since I was in a car, I did NOT get wet, hahaha. I stayed dry the entire 9 day trip, had tunes and Kona Bud and had it made. This was the best car trip I ever took to this day.

I got back into Ellensburg and unloaded the U Haul into the Rental Dump, ready for my new life to start. This picture here shows how classy the furnished dump was. I put the Purple Hair Kona Bud inside that knot hole in the tree trunk, don't ask me why, ha ha-ha. And I had a really nice parking spot for the 74 AMF Chopper, which I hadn't seen for a few days. You can also see my old yeller carpenter tool box and that same buckskin fringe jacket that I got from the base of Pikes Peak on the 1973 Canada Road Trip on the Red 67 Sportster. This was now the end of April, 1980. Time to find a job and some new riding partners.

Chapter 22:

New Guy in Ellensburg

After getting settled in Ellensburg, I flew back to the old home and drove the car up from Dallas, had a place to crash in E-burg and was looking for a carpenter job. Guess what? There weren't none, ha-ha. I had that cuzzin of mine that lived up in Anchorage that first gave me the idea of living up in the mountains, that suggested Ellensburg. He was married and had a son and they sold their house in Anchorage and moved down to Ellensburg. Why?

Cuz his mom in law lived there and she was getting in bad shape with arthritis. Now my cuzzin Joe did the smart thing and also the exact opposite thing of what I did. He sold his house in Alaska where houses are big bucks and he moved to E-burg where houses were cheaper compared to what he had been used to. I sold my cheap house in Dallas and moved to where they cost more. Yikes. I was gettin' in trouble already.

Joe had his builders/contractor's license from Alaska and he got one in Washington pretty fast, he had his tools shipped down and was ready to go. So I went to work for him. But there wasn't much work to be had. Mount Saint Helens blowing up kinda stifled things for a while, too. We got a couple of jobs remodeling kitchens and bathrooms but that was about it, except for 4 houses where we put foundations under them. Joe got hooked up with a real estate guy and in order for the houses to sell in 1980 they had to be up to code. These houses were probably 100 years old or so and did not have foundations. So we'd dig holes under each corner of the house and put concrete blocks in the bottoms of the holes and we'd jack the houses up in the air maybe a foot or so, then dig trenches and pour concrete footings under the perimeter of the house, then lower it back down and bolt it to the new concrete footings. Sounds like fun, eh, It sucked.

In Dallas, 1979, I had been making 12 bucks an hour and my house payment was only 104. I was doing pretty good there. Now I was getting 8 bucks an hour and the rent was double my old house payment. You can see where this is headed,..right? (To the poor house.) But on the fun side, Ellensburg did have some fun bars,...I mean,...taverns,... cuz you couldn't call a drinkin' place a bar there in Washington State. And I fell in with a bunch of good motorsickle people. Dane and Stacy were on their chopped 64 Sportster, Chuck was on his 75 rigid Black Shovel Chopper, Jerry Webb on his Panhead chopper, then there was Ghost Rider Taz and then Mushroom Tim on his Panhead, and Ghost Rider Bob, too, plus a few others.

Now lemme tell ya, being the new young guy in town with the shiny Black Chopper was a horrible thing to have happen to me. Those Ellensburg gals would not leave me alone. It's like they were trying to wear all the skin off my Johnson. Girls from the bars, girls from the diners and cafes, girls from the University, what was a young guy supposed to do, anyhow? I nearly got dehydrated to death.

Now I do have pictures of the Ellensburgers motorsickles, but I didn't get them until 1981, so we will hafta wait a couple of chapters to show them. When our work falls to shit in a few months, I will be moving over the pass to Wenatchee, cuz that is a city with 40,000 people, four times the size of Ellensburg, plus it has a Harley dealer and three cabinet shops to possibly work for. These pictures here are extra random pictures from the 1980 Road Trip to Washington and one photo of the old 1975 Vette parked in front of The Dumpy Crash Pad on Water Street.

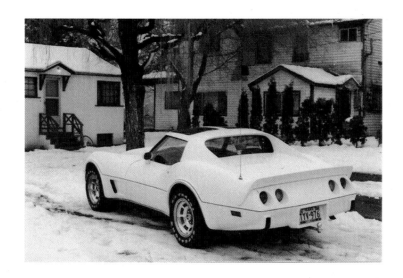

Chapter 23:

THE NIGHT THE 'SPARKS FLEW IN ELLENSBURG.'

The Summer of 1980 in Ellensburg,...after the Mount Saint Helens volcano dust had settled a bit and I got to meet the Ellensburg chopper pilots, I had fun hanging out at the bars with them in Ellensburg's town square. There were actually quite a few bars there for a smaller town. And on nights when we were drinking, we'd have fun going out to the choppers and kicking them over to ride to the next bar, even if the next bar was just across the street or down the block 100 feet. It was fun just making all the racket and causing a ruckus for the citizens. Then one night it got a bit too funny and hairy for me.

We had been out at the First-Last Chance Tavern. The locals called it the First & Last, cuz it had a big lit sign out front that said First Chance Tavern on the side you saw when you were riding into town, and on the other side it said Last Chance Tavern on the side you saw when you were leaving town, so they tried to get you either way,.....and they got me quite a bit with that gimmick, hahaha. After all, here it is 42 years later and I'm still blabbing about it, right?

The group decided our next stop would be the Ugly Bear Tavern and since I knew where that one was, fairly close to the flat I rented on Water Street, I hopped on the 74 AMF Chopper fast, kicked it over, and was the first one to take off. My goal was to beat all the rest of them to the Ugly Bear and get the best-est parking spot, see?

As I pulled away from the group which was still kicking their choppers, I let out a war whoop laugh, shifted gears, popped the foot clutch and took off fast to the Ugly Bear. As I was going through downtown and getting closer, I leaned left going into the corner to turn left at the intersection where the Ugly Bear was. And just as I leaned into the corner good, I noticed in my drunken stupor that some dumb ass rude dump truck had spilled pea gravel in the intersection. But by the time I noticed it, it was already too late.

The rigid chopper started sliding out from under me, the back wheel going out to the right. I knew I was a goner, going down right in front of everybody else that was coming up behind me. How embarrassing. Maybe they'd even run over me, who knows, then somehow while the bike was on its way down to the ground and sliding out from under me, the front wheel turned a bit to the left, which made the right-hand throttle grip go further away from me. And as it got further away, it automatically made me twist the throttle like crazy, but purely by reflex and accident, I had absolutely no control over it. I was like a monkey just riding on top for the ride.

And as the throttle twisted by itself in my hand, the engine revved up and the back wheel spun faster, and to this day I have no idea how it happened, but somehow that back tire bit into the pavement just as the derby cover on the Phase 3 open belt drive was grinding itself into the pavement, throwin' up a shower of sparks in the dark which even I could see off to my left side. It was kinda like fireworks, ha-ha!

So, the chopper righted itself with no help from me, and I nearly had a heart attack as I regained control of the bike and brought it to a stop in front of the Ugly Bear. I backed it into the curb kinda quick pretending like nuthin' had happened, and the others were pulling up next to me yelling out shit like "Hey man! That was fuckin' cool, can ya do it again?" I shut off the chopper, got off and started walking into the tavern on semi-wobbly knees, still kinda shocked from what had just happened. It sobered me up pretty fast, too. So we all went inside and had some more cold frosty beers. So now the Texas stranger in town had a funny story they could tell about him. And that was the night the 'Sparks Flew in Ellensburg.'

Chapter 24:

"THE HI-WAY GRILLE INCIDENT"

Ellensburg Washington, November 1980, 7 of us met up after work at a bar to have a few beers before we went home. You know how that goes,...right? This particular bar was called The Ranch on the outskirts of Ellensburg. Some smart guy had bought a big old barn and fixed it up into the biggest and funnest bar in town. It had a stage in the back for live bands, they had food, good stiff drinks, cold beer, pool tables, big dance floor, a wonderful place we all loved.

It was a jumpin' cold windy Friday night. Next thing we knew it was closing time. So the 7 of us went out to our 6 black Harleys, brushed the light snow off the seats and kicked them over. Ghost Rider Bob and his buddy pulled out first on their Shovels to lead the pack, followed by Dane and Stacy on their chopped 64 Sportster and Mushroom Tim riding next to them on his chopped Panhead. That left Chuck and me riding in the back on our chopped Shovels. Chuck was riding next to the center lane and I was over by the shoulder lane, just puttin' along maybe 35 or 40 mph out in the middle of nowhere, everything totally dark around us except for our headlights, and we're puttin' back to town.

We are headed to The Hi-way Grille for some grub and coffee. Riding along in a pack of 6 bikes, guess what happens next? Yep, red flashing lights pulled up behind Chuck and me in the back of the pack. I looked back over my left shoulder and just then one of the cops hits me with his bright ass spotlight, motioning with it for me to pull over. So I did. I waved Chuck and them on ahead, no use getting the whole pack busted,...right?

So I pulled over onto the side shoulder of the road, hit the toggle switch and shut the 74 AMF Chopper off. No need to advertise the straight exhaust pipes, cuz it's bad enough that I'm still running the Texas license tag and I've been living in Washington now since April,...gulp. The state allowed you 3 months to get a Washington tag and I'd been there for 7 months already, but my Texas sticker was still current. Both cops walk up to me, first one asks "Do you know why we pulled you over?" Me,..."Nope. We weren't speeding, were we?" The cop sez "Your tail light is burned out." I said "Oh really? Well, it was working earlier tonight when I got gas, lemme see if it works now."

Back then I did not run a battery, I used those Sebring Battery Eliminators, so that means the lights would not work unless the motor was running. So next I'm getting ready to kick it over right in front of them to test the tail light. I was standing on the carb side of the bike, leaned across, flipped the toggle switch back on, pulled the kicker out and put my foot on it. Then I jumped up into the air a bit to kick down on the 86 inch motor, and when I got to the bottom of the kick stroke, my drunk foot slipped off the pedal, the kicker arm came slamming back up, the bike lurched forward some, the kick stand folded, and the handle bars slipped outta my drunk hands and I dropped the newly built chopper right in front of both cops, with it crashing down on its left primary side. Oh shit. This is not good, is it?

One of the cops looked at me and asked "Exactly how much have you had to drink tonight?" I sez "I ain't gonna lie, officer, I had a whole lot more beers than I intended to. We were headed up to The Hi-way Grille to get some food and coffee." And just as I bent over to pick the 74 Chopper up, the other cop actually helped me lift it back up and put it back on the kick stand, Then the other cop sez "You head on up the road with your buddies and we'll stay behind you so nobody runs over you from behind."

And that's how I got a nice Reverse Police Escort back to town. And once I got there, the others could not believe the story, but there I was, right in front of them, not in jail and got no ticket. And that is the only time cops were ever nice to me and I still owe them two guys a big thanks,.....and some beers.

Chapter 25:

GHOST OF CHRISTMAS PAST

Ellensburg Washington 1980.

And this is where Mister Chuck Larimer comes into play. It was Christmas Eve, 40 years ago. Chuck and Jodi and Dane and Stacy and a few others of us had been out semi terrorizing the bars, trying to drink up all the Jack Daniels and beer in town.

For Christmas Eve dinner I remember I feasted on Fried Clam Strips and tartar sauce out at one of the bars, maybe The Ugly Bear? Anyhow we'd drink at one bar, then go out into the cold and kick over the choppers and ride off to another bar. I'll bet you mighta done that once or twice before your own self,...right? It's fun.

Anyway, we were having fun drinking, smokin' some green stuff, shootin' pool and playin' pinball and what have you and next thing ya know, it was kinda late and the bars were closing.

Since I had the dump right around the corner, I invited all my new pals back for some more fun cuz I had bottles of Jack and beer there, plus some weed hidden in that tree stump that I kept inside the living room......why not?

So we got to the point where shot glasses weren't needed anymore, just sluggin' down the bottle of Jack and chasing it with beer. I remember Dane and Stacy looking at me kinda in half disgust and half disbelief, saying shit like "I don't see how you can keep drinking whiskey like that." So I told them in my Big Mouth Texas Style, "Well I am from Texas and I guess we drink more than you folks do up here." And, knowing me like I do, I probably burped at them, ha-ha.

One by one and two by two, the chopper ridin' partiers drifted off to their own places, and I was left standing in the back doorway facing Rossow's Burgers waving goodbye to Chuck and Jodi, cuz they were the last ones leaving.

No sooner had they rode away, that fuckin' room started spinning and next thing I knew I was pukin' my guts up. Up came all the whiskey that I had paid good money for, up came all the beer. Up came all the Fried Clam Strips, oh no, there went my din din.

I headed into the only bedroom and flopped down on the bed, only to have the room start spinning. So I did my old Dallas Spinning Room Trick, and I put my foot down on the floor beside the bed to stop the room from spinning.

Somehow the Dallas Spinning Room Trick had no effect up there in Volcano Land Washington. And up I went back to the bathroom to puke some more. I puked and puked, then I puked some more. I jumped into the shower, went back to bed, and got up and ran to the bathroom and puked some more.

This was the most I ever threw up in my life. Merry Christmas. Not only did I throw up everything in my belly that had gone down there the past 48 hours, I got into the Stomach Bile Puke Stage. That is where you throw up that stuff that looks like a mixture of mustard and honey, but it smells worse. I think I mighta even threw up chunks of small intestine, but I can't swear to it cuz I was drunk.

Anyhow, that experience stopped me from drinking whiskey for almost 12 years. I could not even stand to smell a bottle cap off a bottle of Jack, and that had been my favorite thing to drink.

Oh well, just thought I'd share some pleasant memories from Christmas of 40 years ago. Merry Christmas, and don't drink too much or you might be typing up one of these sad stories to share.

Right after I got to Ellensburg, that Mount Saint Helens blew her top, and that's about the time I met Mister Chuck Larimer and his band of chopper pilots. I could not have found a better group of people to stumble into. They were instant kindred souls.

I landed a job as a carpenter working on peoples' houses and did some light commercial work. I got a cheap seedy furnished flat that was a side-by-side duplex right on the Main Drag of E-burg, across the street from Rossow's Burgers joint. I had the Hi-Way Grill down to my left, and all the bars right in the neighborhood.

The best thing about the seedy flat was it had indoor parking. At this stage, the 74 AMF still has bead blasted lower legs, black triple trees, and the funny attempt I made at a tail light and license tag bracket. And no front brake, which was also illegal. I even yanked off the front fender after I got there, just used it for the ride up from Dallas.

Now Chuck can fill in the details better than I can, cuz he knew the area people and their stories. And even at this early stage, I was already being pressured by The Man in E-burg to get a Washington license tag for the chopper. But I was a-skeered to, cuz of this story Chuck and Dane told me.

Chuck and Dane said they knew of a guy there in E-burg who painstakingly built up a really nice Panhead over several months. When he got the Pan finished, he took it down to The Man to get the Official Inspection so he could get the license tag on back. But guess what The Man did?

They impounded the Panhead, saying some parts on it looked suspicious, like they may have been stolen. So, they kept the guy's Pan for several weeks. Eventually, the cops admitted they did not find anything they could prove was stolen, so they gave the Panhead back to the poor guy.................in boxes. Now do ya see why I didn't wanna go get a state inspection? That Panhead guy was born and raised there, and I was an out of stater. Just imagine what they coulda/woulda done to me?

Anyhow, here's my cheap-o seedy flat in E-burg where I had indoor parking. And there's the buckskin fringe jacket that I got back in 1973 when I rode up Pikes Peak. I lived here in this nice dump until December 1981. Then I found an indoor job in a nice warm cabinet shop over The Hump in Wenatchee, so I moved there January 1, 1981.

Early 1980s story time and this time we have Chuck for a witness. There was this Washington State Patrol trooper that hated choppers. As a matter of fact, anyone who ever went into their headquarters in Wenatchee would see a nice life size mural on their back wall, of 2 nice squad cars who had pulled over a chopper and were hassling the guy. Anyhow, on to the story.

This one trooper was named Truman Douglas. I found out his first name through my boss at work when I got a job there in January 1981. This was a few months before the homeless days, cuz I had my own apartment then.

Asshole Truman Douglas would pull your chopper over any and every time he saw you, it seemed to me.

Chuck was mentioning the Highway 97 that runs over Blewett Pass, and Truman would hang out on that stretch of road waiting to nab any chopper that dared ride from Ellensburg to Wenatchee, or out to Leavenworth, see?

I still had my Texas driver's license and license tag on the 74 AMF. Truman did not like that. He would pull me over and yell at me for no front brake, only 1 rear view mirror, loud pipes, shit like that, just to pester me and pass his time of day.

When you ride over Blewett Pass, Highway 97 dumps you off and then you take Route 22 into Wenatchee through a little town called Cashmere.

One day I saw Asshole Truman Douglas in his squad car waaaaay up the hill, sitting in his usual spot just off the right-side shoulder of the road where he could get speeding cars and me. On the side of the highway there is the river that was the Icicle which flowed into the Columbia on down the line, and there is also a service road that the apple and cherry farmers use to get to their places.

I downshifted, pulled off the highway and hit the little bridge going over the river, which put me on the service road. Then I twisted the throttle and took off up the road, nice and loud.

In about 1/4 mile or so I saw Truman, and I was riding nice and loud and speeding, and there wasn't one damn thing he could do about it, cuz the river was between him and me, bwah ha-ha.

He jumped in his squad car and took off up the highway and caught up to me, but we were on different roads. Then he turned his squad car lights and siren on and took off up the highway to head me off at the pass.

So, at the next rounded bend in the little service road, I did a U-turn and headed back the direction I had come. He did not get me that day, but he was really pissed off the next time he pulled me over. And I swear that fucker musta pulled me over 15 to 18 times in the 8 months I lived there, bah ha-ha.

OK, now here's some pictures from back then. We got Tiny's Fruit Stand on the side of that road in Cashmere, and Tiny standing next to his Cadillac, and an apple orchard photo.

Chapter 26:

HEADED FOR WENATCHEE

Although I loved Ellensburg and the motorsickle folks I met there, I was sinking fast. I was making 2/3rds the pay I made in Dallas the year before and my rent was double what my old house payment was. So do the math and I'm in big trouble.

One fine cold Saturday, Dane came by in his late 1950s Chevy Panel Wagon, and he had his 64 Sportster motor in the back and Chuck and Tim inside, so I jumped in. We were headed off on Highway 97 across Blewett Pass to Wenatchee cuz there was an old timer there named Jim who did outstanding motor jobs and he was gonna do Dane's 64 Ironhead motor. I was just sittin' in the back seat listening to them talk and the tunes and I was keeping the joints rolling.

When we got into Wenatchee, I was surprised, cuz it was about 4 times the size of Ellensburg. E-burg was around 10,000 population back then and Wenatchee was around 40,000. It also had a Harley dealer, who also split the shop as a Kawasaki dealer, but at least I could get 50 weight oil there. We saw Jim and dropped off Dane's motor, then headed back over the pass to Ellensburg. Work for me had been really slow, which = no work-ie no pay-ie. So I made a trip back over to Wenatchee a coupla days later to check it out for myself, thinking maybe I'd move there. And I did.

I talked to a cabinet shop there, told the guy I had completed a 4 year apprenticeship, had my journeyman's papers, and the guy offered me a job. They worked 4 days a week, 10 hours a day. I could roll with that, 3 day weekends alla time. Only problem was the pay. The guy who ran the sop was named Jack. He told me since he didn't know me from Adam and since I had zero references for work, he'd start me out at 6 bucks an hour,.....yikes. But he also said after I'd been there for a month or two and worked out OK, he'd give me a raise. So I went for it. At least cabinet shops are warm in the winter to work in. So I made the move to Wenatchee and moved into a rental house on the east side of town which was 300 bucks a month, ouch! It was about the same size house as mine in Dallas, and it also had an attached garage.

Here's the 74 AMF Chopper overlooking the big ass Columbia River, which is the border between Washington and Oregon.

So now I'm working for half what I made in Dallas the year before but at least my rent is triple what my old house payment was, In other words, I'm headed down to the Poor House fast.

That shop worked 4 days a week, 10 hour days and they paid you every other week. So in the middle of January when I got my first paycheck, I tagged along to Joe's Log Cabin Tavern with the rest of the work crew to cash our paychecks drink some beer and shoot pool. There was no such thing as ATMs back then and the banks were closed by the time we got off work, and besides, banks didn't have cold beer, fried clam strips and pool tables anyhow, ha ha-ha.

So we are cashing our checks with Joe, and when I cashed mine and Joe gave me the pile of cash, the other guys kinda looked at me funny. Jim with the 75 Sportster said "Damn! How much are you getting paid?" I thought he was kinda feeling sorry for me cuz Jack the Boss Man had told me the guys in his shop made around 10, 12, and 14 bucks an hour. I said "Jack's paying me 6 bucks an hour, why?" Jim sez, "Holy shit, I've been there for 2 years now and I get $6.50 an hour." Then Dan chimed in and said he only got 5 bucks an hour. So I found out on that very spot that instead of being the lowest paid guy in the shop like I thought I was, I was actually the 3rd highest paid, out of a crew of 12 guys, which made me feel kinda shitty, ya know? So it is a starvation type of sweat shop, bwah a ha-ha, and now I'm caught up in the middle of it, with no place to escape to. Holy shit.

So I hung onto the job, eatin' sawdust with no chance of a raise in the foreseeable future. But at least I was living in the mountains and seeing new sights on my chopper rides,.....right? Say yes, to make me feel better, ha ha-ha. Meanwhile, I am beginning to realize Randal mighta made the right choice staying in Dallas, cuz he still has his decent paying job as a Detroit Diesel Mechanic.

Here is the 74 AMF Chopper in front of the little house I rented in East Wenatchee, in spring 1981, and I'm gonna throw in three extra shots showing how purdy that area is, a water falls, the view from up on top of the ridge overlooking Wenatchee, and a forest growing right out of old Volcano lava

Chapter 27:

EAST WENATCHEE RIDING

After I discovered that out of a crew of 12 guys, I was the 3rd highest paid carpenter in the cabinet shop at a measley 6 bucks an hour. Things were going downhill fast. I stayed in that rental house from January to May, then Jim who rode the 75 Sportster said an apartment in his building called The Columbia Arms opened up, so I moved in kinda close to him and Debbie. At least I had some new friends to hang with in this new town, and they both liked to ride, toke and drink, ha-ha ha. Natural born riding friends.

I was still hanging onto the old 75 Vette, but I could see the writing on the wall that it would soon be gone. But on the good side, look at the great parking spot the 74 AMF Chopper got. When I'd come in on it, I'd shut the motor off out in the parking lot, and then I had a downhill sidewalk coast going from the parking lot right up to my front door, I could sneak it in and out of that apartment without the landlady ever finding out. Pushing it back up the sidewalk to leave wasn't exactly my favorite part though.

The rent house had a nice garage, this place did not, but it did have two bedrooms which meant I could keep all my boxes of extra bike parts like the busted Durfee girder inside the place, so I didn't hafta rent a storage unit. And it was kinda party central here, lots of young folks, and it had a nice big swimming pool with a diving board which meant lots of bikinis hanging around, about 50 steps from my front door. How convenient, eh? And I had a nice view of Mission Ridge to look at so I could watch the sun set over the mountains while I was firing up the Weber grill, which you can see in the picture, and it's also inside that apartment.

So, moving into the 2-bedroom apartment in East Wenatchee, where it was kinda party central for the whole building. In other words, it wasn't a retirement home just yet.

Now the bad thing about working 10 hour days every week is it can get tiresome standing on concrete all damn day, but the good thing is we always had 3 day weekends. So what's a 25 year old whippersnapper to do with himself and his freshly built Black Hot Rod Chopper on 3 day weekends in his new beautiful home state? Why go riding all around it and see the things Texas never had. Like lush forests, roads winding through beautiful mountains with no traffic, the Pacific Ocean, rivers pouring right outta the sides of mountains as you ride by.

I rode over the beautiful North Cascade Highway, which they call State Route 20 that goes through little mountain towns like Winthrop and takes you close to Mount Baker, and I'd ride over to the ocean and around the Olympic Peninsula, where ever I felt like wandering. Washington may be a smaller state but it is filled with lots of nice places to ride.

Here are a few shots of Washington's nice countryside I took while riding the 74 AMF Chopper around mountain passes and North Cascade Highway. One Thursday night in the spring of 1981, I packed the road gear on the chopper in order to get a really early start for Friday morning, cuz I had planned to ride over to see the ocean. The town I picked out was Aberdeen. Not too many people had probably heard of Aberdeen until a rock & roll guy named Kurt Cobain announced that he came from there a few years later. It is a really nice little town sitting right on the ocean.

So early that Friday morning I pushed the loaded chopper outta the apartment and up the sidewalk to the parking lot, kicked the chopper over and headed out on Highway 97 over the 4,000 foot summit of Blewett Pass to Ellensburg, then cut out onto I-90 to make some time. The deal is, when you are riding someplace in Washington, on the map it will show it ain't that many miles, but the way you gotta get there is like riding in Colorado, lots of switchbacks and up and down and in and out winding, so it can take you a coupla hours to go even 50 miles sometimes. That's why I went with I-90 to Aberdeen. It probably took me about 5 hours to get there, most of the day's ride.

I remember having fresh hot clam chowder and cold Rainier beer,...again,...at one of those things they called 'grottos' along the beach. I found a place on the edge of town to pitch the tent for the night and crashed.

When I woke up early the next morning, I saw the moon hidin' in clouds over the ocean, and it was shining down on the ocean and beach, kinda like a reverse sunset type of thing. So I took this picture here which has turned out to be one of my favorite pictures I ever took, and it was by accident, bwah a ha-ha. That's the best way sometimes. I had the camera set up to take a regular boring picture of the moon shining down on the ocean and beach, nice and calm like. And then just as I snapped the shutter on the Canon, that dumb ol' bird flew in front of the moon and this is what happened. So here it is, my favorite picture, to you from Aberdeen, spring of 1981.

I was just riding around the Washington State coast taking it all in. The 3-day weekends really were fun, cuz I went riding somewhere camping every weekend. And the good thing about camping in Washington State was I never saw any 'skeeters. That's right. And the places there that I lived in didn't even have screens on their windows cuz there weren't that many bugs. Now being I'm from Dallas, I was used to bugs and 'skeeters like crazy, hahaha, so this was a nice change to not get bit while camping. Seems there were always nice campgrounds right next to rivers and streams. It was heaven to go riding through.

Here's three more photos, a trail in the woods, a big ass mountain sticking up, and for all you folks who eat apples, check the tag on the next apple you eat and see if it sez 'Wenatchee Washington' on it, cuz this is where most of 'em come from. So here's you an Official Apple Orchard picture from Wenatchee. There are tons of these orchards up and down the highways and all over the hills, plus cherry orchards, peaches, and pears. Apple Blossom is a huge festival in Wenatchee that gets lots of bikes every year...or at least it used to.

Chapter 28:

WENATCHEE WASHINGTON SUMMER 1981

W e left off last time having fun riding and camping all over the state of Washington enjoying those 3 day weekends. Also, in my spare time I had made myself a really nice carpenter tool box out of Koa Wood, from Hawaii. I wanted a nice tool box not only to keep my tools in, but to also use like a rolling business card, to try to impress upon these strangers that I could actually do woodwork, cuz nobody knew me there, hahaha.

Washington had a really beautiful landscape to ride in, but what they didn't have very many of was,...........jobs. There wasn't any Microsoft crap going on, Boeing was laying people off by the hunnerds, Starbucks had just been started a few years earlier in 1977, I think it was. On Fridays sometimes I made pilgrimages from Wenatchee to Seattle looking for construction work. What did I find in Seattle? Only 2 or 3 buildings going up and those jobs had these huge ass 4 foot x 8 foot plywood signs up at the job gate which said "NOT HIRING". Hmm. In other words, there wasn't any plentiful work like I had in Texas when it had been booming. And then it happened,.....the shit hit the fan.

Half of us in the shop got laid off and that meant me, cuz I was the last guy hired. Fuck. Now what? I sold the ol' White '75 Vette, sniff, sniff, rented a storage unit in Wenatchee and stuffed my boxes of chopper parts, stereo, albums, TV, clothes, the new tool box, and kitchen crap into the storage unit. I paid the guy 6 months rent up front cuz I didn't know what the future held. It was the end of August now. So instead of staying in town with no jobbie job and paying rent with no pay check coming in, I signed up for unemployment, used a friend's address for the check to get mailed to, and then I decided to go Full Time Camping.......

So now I lived in the woods. No more taking 3-day weekend chopper trips around the state, cuz now I lived on the chopper. I also ditched my old orange pup tent and got a nice green and yeller tent with more room. See if you can spy it here at my new home up by The Icicle River outside Leavenworth in the center of the state? I'd park the chopper in those woods next to the tent and I leaned it up against the trees cuz the kick stand would sink in the soft ground covered with pine needles.

So being homeless and jobless, but not fun-less. I was still hanging on to the riding and camping life on the trusty 74 AMF Chopper which I had built in my living room back in Dallas the year before. I'd ride where ever I wanted, and I'd camp at Icicle River most of the time. But I would also venture over to Lake Chelan and camp there, and camp at Box Canyon Creek Campground. Or I could swing back up by Wintrop on the North Cascade Highway and camp up there. I had some nice spots picked out around the state and I'd go between them. It might sound crazy and hectic, but looking back, this was one of the most enjoyable times of my 67 years on this planet.

The only deal was, I had to be back in Wenatchee every other week to get the unemployment check cashed and fill out the paperwork for the next 2 weeks, hahaha. And this was back when you had to go in person and beg for it. How humiliating, eh? But it kept me going. We all gotta eat some dirt once in a while. Gulp.

Yep, it was a tranquil peaceful life,..so far. But,.....what comes after fall? Winter? Another yep. And there was no way in hell I wanted to be living in a tent come winter time in Washington, brrrr-ha ha-ha. So, I made the plan to leave. Going back to Dallas for some work. Randal and me had a friend who had a Black 75 Sportster named Gary and now he was a carpenter foreman and could help me out with some work. I left my new tool box in the storage unit in Wenatchee cuz my dad was also a carpenter and he had enough tools and tool boxes for me to borrow to work on the job. I could just picture my dad,.....saying shit like,.....Oh great, here comes my prodigal son, blew all his house money and now he's coming back begging for work, ha ha ha! True,....true...... This picture is out on the road headed back to Dallas now.

Chapter 29:

FALL 1981, BECOMING A CHOPPER HOBO

Recap,... got laid off from the cabinet shop, sold the ol' 75 Vettte, signed up for unemployment with checks to be mailed to my friend's house in Wenatchee, moved outta the fun apartment and stuck everything in a storage unit in Wenatchee, lived on the chopper and the new green & yeller tent from the end of August to the beginning of November. Then I loaded up the chop for the road and took off back to Dallas to lick my wounds and try to regroup. I had a carpenter job waiting for me in Dallas working for my old 75 Sportster riding partner Gary, who was also pals with Randal.

This was a fun fall ride, 2,000 miles, kinda semi-boring cuz nothing happened breakdown-wise, no big rain storms, and I didn't meet anybody on a chopper out on the road. Riding back through eastern Washington and Idaho was still kinda new to me, but by this time I knew Montana, Wyoming, Colorado and New Mexico like the back of my hand, cuz of the cross-country trips I had taken through there in 1973, 74, 75, 78, and 79. I could almost put the 74 AMF Chopper on Automatic Pilot, sit back and enjoy the ride.

I rode on I-90 through eastern Washington and acrost the top of Idaho, then stayed on it through the western part of Big Sky Country Montana. After riding east through Billings, I took the split off from I-90 to I-25 and rode south through Wyoming and down through Colorado, into Raton New Mexico, where I jumped over to my ol' buddy, Highway 287. I averaged around 500 miles a day cuz I made the trip in 4 days flat. Since I gave you the 'moonrise' photo up in Aberdeen Washington

I'd taken a few weeks before, this here is a sunset photo out on the spacious road,...
somewhere,... don't remember exactly where I took this one, ha ha-ha.

Chapter 30:

Fall 1981, Now a Chopper Hobo

Left off last time in November riding from Washington State back to Dallas where I had a job waiting. At this time I was now officially homeless, no address, no phone, no nuthin', but I did still have some cash from selling the 75 Vette, so I wasn't dead broke down and out, hah. And the rest of my stuff was in a storage unit in Wenatchee Washington.

I had another important reason to get back to Dallas and that reason was the license tag sticker. Yep, the Texas tag was becoming a huge issue for the Washington State Patrol in Wenatchee, especially one Office Truman Douglas, who was a total asshole. He pulled me over every time he saw me, out of boredom I suppose. One of the older guys I worked with back at the cabinet shop had gone to high school with Truman and told me what a prick he was even in high school. So I had some fun with that. He'd pull me over and I'd say "Howdy there Truman, how are you doing this fine morning?" Shit like that.

Anyhow, the deal was, Washington State demanded you get one of their license tags and title for your vehicle if you fall under 2 Conditions: If you have a job working in the state and have been there over 3 months, you must get a Washington license tag and title, Weird, eh? Or if you have kids going to a school there, they consider that to make you a citizen of the state as well.

But I did not fall into either category. I didn't have a job anymore and I didn't have kids in their schools. I'd simply tell Truman Douglas that I was there on 'extended vacation' and was still a Texas citizen with a Texas Driver's License, Texas title and Texas license tag on the chopper and I did not hafta conform to his rules. That really pissed him off, cuz I was correct.

Anyhow, that is the background for why I gotta get a new Texas license tag sticker, cuz mine is expiring at this stage, ha ha-ha. I used my folks' address and got the new sticker for like $5.30 or something like that, maybe it had gone up to 7 bucks by then? anyhow, now I was safe for another year, no matter where I roamed. I still have that license tag up on the wall in the garage, along with all the other tags from other states that chopper has run over the decades.

The job my buddy had waiting for me was installing the baseboards in Red Bird Mall in South Dallas. Yep, that's right, installing base, crawling on my hands and knees all damn day, ha ha-ha. Down on the floor where people spit, and where the cockroaches and mouse turds were. But it was a paycheck, right? So in a matter of 4 days on the road riding down, I had now gone from riding the chopper and living in a tent in beautiful peaceful quiet Washington State to horrible bumper to bumper freeway traffic in Dallas.

My dad had his 1969 Chevy pick up he loaned me while I was there for the winter weeks, and I crashed at various places, always trying to be a nice guest by buying food, booze, or weed for the friends who were kind enough to put me up. And to occupy some more time, I decided it was time for an upgrade on the 74 AMF Chopper, which was still less than 1 year along on its total rebuild. This early morning picture here sez it is 75 miles to Fort Worth. And this is the last photo I have of the 74 AMF Chopper looking like this. Some new front end work is coming up.So crawlin' all damn day on your hands and sore knees putting down wood baseboards on a hard parquet floor in a huge shopping mall ain't no picnic, but it was a paycheck. I was working in Dallas now, got the new license tag sticker for the Texas license plate, was visiting family and friends over the holidays, having a pretty good time being back in my old stomping grounds where I was raised.

And then there was the 74 AMF Chopper lookin' at me. It had performed flawlessly since its new bare frame up build in December of 1979. The Joe Cox stroker motor was awesome, nice and powerful with no oil leaks and no breakdowns out on the road where I was depending on it to take care of me, haha. My molding job on the frame was still holding up good and the Black Imron Paint that Terry had sprayed during the last build was still just as shiny as black glass. So it was time to change it up some,...right?

I rode the Shovelhead over to my folks' house, lifted and braced the frame and pulled the wide glide off. I scuffed up the chrome front fender I had gotten at Brown's Custom Cycles a few years earlier and gave it to Terry to paint Black Imron, along with the lower legs which had been bead blasted during the last build. And I gave Terry my home-made bracket for mounting the front fender so he could spray it black, too. Then I went over to Shelby's shop Mid Cities Choppers and he sold me a Panhead front brake drum, backing plate, the guts inside, and that funnel shaped tube that holds the front brake cable. I took the brake parts and tube and the two swap meet triple trees over to the chrome shop in Dallas to get made shiny. They did them fast.

Meanwhile, I was working on tidying up other areas of the chopper and I remodeled the back end some. I got rid of the bracket I had used for a few years that held the tail light and license tag. I drilled and bottom tapped 4 holes in the back of the sissy bar to make a nice sturdy clean mount for the Knight light and tag, and then redid the wiring some back there.

When the chrome and paint were done, I put it back together and rode it over to the Harley dealer in Arlington where Joe Cox worked, cuz they were having a swap meet and sale that weekend and Doctor Burns the Emergency Pin Striper was gonna be on hand. I was now gonna get the chopper pin striped in red, to match the red crushed velvet on the swap meet Drag Specialties Butt Bucket seats. How fuckin' classy, eh?

At the swap meet in Arlington, I finally got to meet Doctor Burns. He dressed in white like a medic and he traveled in a white van that he had fixed up to look like an ambulance. Maybe some of you Texas folks have heard of him? Anyhow, he laid out the red lines on the chopper which elevated it to a new level,....in my opinion, any-how, hah aha ha, So this is the new look for the 74 AMF Chopper for January 1982.

a newer look, some chrome action, Black Imron paint by Terry and red pin stripes by Doctor Burns Emergency Pin Striping. Here's some more pictures of his fine work and the new updated look for the front end.

Chapter 31:

MARCH 1982, A CHOPPER HOBO

To recap, after going flat broke in Washington State and having to sell the car, I stuck my stuff in a storage unit and rode the 74 AMF Chopper back down to Dallas to regroup and lick my wounds, Did couch surfing between friends, visited the family some, did the little upgrades on the Chopper's wide glide and got a job installing lots of base board in the Red Bird Mall in South Dallas, crawling on my hands and knees all day for around 3 months. But all good things and even bad things eventually come to an end, and so did that job, whether it was good or bad,... who knows? It was a pay check and I was able to stash a few bucks away. That was the main goal.

Now, at this time, you might think a normal person would be satisfied with stashing a bit of cash from the Red Bird Mall job and might actually look for a place to live in Dallas and get another construction job. A normal person might even realize things were not all that good job-wise in Washington. A normal person might try to regroup in Dallas where his life long friends were. But nobody ever accused me of being normal, bwah a ha-ha.

So what did I do? Why I stuffed my meager road belongings I had with me into the duffelbag for the road, tied the tent and sleeping bag on the Chopper, said farewell to everybody and took off for Wenatchee Washington again, ha ha-ha. Call me a glutton for punishment?

I left Dallas the beginning of March, 1982 with my brand new updated Texas license tag sticker, mind you, and lemme tell ya, that ain't exactly the best time of year to be riding cross country. It was cold as fuck. I froze my ass off. I also stayed in motels all four nights on the road so's I could take hot showers. I'll be damned if I'm camping out in that cold shit after riding in it all damn day. I had the bucks, so it was no big deal.

The fifth night I finally got into Wenatchee around sunset, rode right downtown and got a room in The Chieftain Motel, right on the main drag. I even told them I wanted a room for 2 nights and not to wake me up the next morning for check out time. So after the office guy gave me the room key, I rode the Chopper further into the parking lot back next to the room and hauled my gear inside and locked up the bike. Then I jumped in that hot shower and stayed until I turned into a fuckin' wrinkly raisin. After I got out, I put on fresh clothes and walked right into their fancy restaurant like I owned the joint.

I got a little table over by the bar and already knew what to order. They make a really good starter salad with their own house made dressing and it comes with warm Apple Bread fresh outta their oven, any of you that have been there know exactly what I'm talking about. After that, next came the big ass fuckin' Prime Rib with Horseradish and a baked potato, washed it all down with icy cold Rainier Beer, and after that, warm apple pie out of their oven with vanilla ice cream. Yep, I ate every bit of that, stuffed myself to the gills then went back to the room and crashed until the next day around noon. I'd worry about tomorrow when tomorrow got there.

This picture here is back in Wenatchee, up on the ridge. It's in the same spot cuz that was my spot where I'd ride up and look out over the valley and smoke weed with no cops around. In this picture you can see the lower legs and front fender are now black, there is a chrome Panhead front brake, and the triple trees are chrome since the last time you all seen this bike in this spot before so it is a new picture.

Chapter 32:

ABATE SPRING OPENER

Left off last time in March riding the 74 AMF Chopper from Dallas back up to Wenatchee Washington. I was crashing on different folks' couches in Wenatchee, and luckily I had made a few friends there the year before, so I could spread myself kinda thin and not hafta stay at any one place for too long,....and that was good, hahaha.

One of the first guys I talked to was a guy named Kenny and he was an outside contractor who did installation work for the old cabinet shop I used to work at, the one that laid 6 of us off the previous fall. Kenny had landed a nice contract doing interior woodwork at some condos they were building on the Wenatchee Country Club grounds, ooh la la. And he offered me a job at 9 bucks an hour doing,.......guess what? Installing cherry baseboards, bwahahaha. So after crawling on my hands and knees in Dallas for 3 months doing base at Red Bird Mall, now I can do some more base here. But hey, it's all part of the trade, so I didn't whine. And since I kept my mouth shut and just did the work, later on he let me do some kitchen cabinets and countertops, too, and then some doors and hardware, so it was all good.

So what's the next fun thing to come up in Washington State, bike-wise? Why the ABATE Washington Spring Opener, that's what. So of course, I went. And by this time, the weather was letting up some and I could stop couch surfing and started living in the tent up on Icicle River. When the Spring Opener came around, all I had to do was ride up Highway 97 over Blewett Pass and take a right turn to the campground.

This picture here is out in the middle of the action in the woods at the 1982 ABATE Spring Opener. And it looks like there is an old chopper out in the middle that looks kinda familiar to me. Why yes, it is,. It's that ol' 74 AMF Shovel Chopper that rode up from Dallas, and it won 3rd Place in this Ride In Bike Show, got a case of Rainier Beer for the prize and we drank it all up,....burp. The bronze colored Panhead Chopper on the left got 2nd Place and 1st Place went to a beautiful restored Indian Chief, but it was over on the other side of the pile of bikes so it ain't in this picture.

OK here's another ultra excitin' shot from the 1982 ABATE Washington Spring Opener, showing the nice parking spots my ridin' buddies and me got, right in front of our tents. And I don't wanna make anybody all jealous an' shit now, but there on the left side of this picture is my fancy new green and yeller tent. That's right, the little orange pup tent is long gone now and this green one is my new home on the road. What happened to the little orange pup tent that served me well since the 1973 Road Trip to Canada? I was riding west on I-84 by The Dalles in northern Oregon and I hit a few small bumps, and I noticed the little orange tent was coming loose rolled up inside the middle of the sleeping bag on the front fender. It kinda worried me a little bit, but I thought I could fix it at the next gas station,...right? So I kept on ridin' down the road.

But then another bigger bump came up, and it knocked the tent outta the sleeping bag and the tent fell off to the left side of me on the road, and I was in the left side of the right hand lane, and there was an 18 wheeler in the left lane and he ran over my little orange pup tent and he kilt it plumb daid,.....sniff, sniff. The truck destroyed the tent poles, flattened them out like a road kill squirrel, and the tent itself got ripped to shreds. How do I know all of this? Cuz I turned around to go back to see if it was OK. It was not OK. I shoulda taken a picture of it dead on the road, but I was too sad. If ya ask me, very few things are sadder than a homeless chopper hobo losing his little pup tent home. So this green one is its new replacement.

Here's another picture from the 1982 ABATE Spring Opener Run in Washington. I will also add that back then, ABATE stood for A Brotherhood Against Totalitarian Enactments, as in against the mandatory helmet laws, not the American Bikers Aimed Toward Education it became later on. You can see the band on stage in the background, and this was back when most bikers were into rock & roll, not the candy ass stuff the record industry tries to pass off as country music these days, hahaha.

Pictures can be funny and time can be weird. See that little kid that's kinda bow-legged with his back to the camera? He's probably in his early 50s today and maybe he's been riding for 30 years now.

I was a member of ABATE when I lived in Dallas in the 1970s. We rode to Daytona as a group and camped at New Smyrna Beach KOA with all the other ABATE Chapters. And the chapter from South Carolina was our neighbors in the campground. I remember one guy named Possum that rode a stroker Knuckle and he told me that he made his cool push rod covers out of VW parts, if anybody out there remembers him or that campground.

After the ABATE Spring Opener a few of us gathered at The Brick Saloon in Roslyn for some 'brewskis', as I heard a few guys in that area call them. The Brick Saloon is allegedly the oldest tavern in the entire state. And it was inside The Brick that I saw one of the earliest forms of a urinal. There was a hole in the back wall where a little stream from outside came in through the wall in the back of the building.

That little stream then ran in a brass gutter type of thing in front of the bar down under your feet underneath the ancient brass foot rail. When you needed to take a leak, you simply whooped it out and just did it, then the water in the brass gutter ran the used beer outside the front wall into the street. Don't ask me what the ladies did cuz I dunno.

And it was here in The Brick Saloon that I met my first real life Train Tramp. I was already sittin' on the bar stool when this smaller guy with a full head of snow white hair and beard came in and asked if I minded if he sat next to me. I said not at all, have a seat pal.

He set his bag behind us up against the wall, hopped up on the bar stool, said thanks for the offer, then stuck out his hand and said "My name's Whitey and I ride the High Line." I said 'Nice to meet you, Whitey, my name's Dave and what's the High Line?" He said "That's what us railroad tramps call the Burlington Northern, cuz it runs up here in the high mountains."

So naturally I asked "Is there also a Low Line?" He laughed and said "Yes, and the Low Line is the Southern Pacific that runs down south. I ride the High Line when I want to and then I ride the Low Line mostly in winter." And that's how this Chopper Hobo met the real Train Hobo. These pictures are from that day. Wish I'da gotten one of Whitey, he was really cool looking.

These are in front of The Brick Saloon, with Dane's Panhead and the 74 AMF Chop on the end, and then a look across the street at some more bikes.

When the weekend was over and all the folks went back to their homes and jobs, I rode back to a little lake over by Leavenworth and set up the tent again for my home.

Chapter 33:

May 1982, a Chopper Hobo's Cursed Month

We left off last time where I actually had a job working for Kenny getting 9 whole bucks an hour,...yay. That carpenter job came to an end in April when it was finished. So I rode down to the Unemployment Office in Wenatchee and signed up, using my buddy Reed's address and phone number, since I still didn't have either. Kenny my carpenter boss buddy graciously hauled my tool box in his van back over to my little storage unit in East Wenatchee and now I was living in the tent again out on the Icicle River. Things were going OK.

Then came the cursed month of May. I rode in from the Icicle to Reed's place to get the Unemployment Check, and it was not there. So I started to ride back out to the river around sundown. I was riding down a road I think they called River Road, cuz it was winding along the river on the edge of town with houses on both sides. It was a 2 lane black top road with the white stripes down the middle, you know the type, and it was a fun ride, cruisin' along around 40 or so,.....ain't got no speedo to tell for sure.

Suddenly this dirty filthy tan VW Bug comes up from behind me with no lights on, going pretty fast. It whipped out to the left of me and passed me in the oncoming traffic's lane, and as it passed, I saw there were 2 little teeny bopper girls in the VW Bug which was covered with dirt, mud, bird shit and no license tag when it went by me. It looked like they just untombed it from the junk yard. Oh well, no big deal. But then the next thing I saw was a big deal, cuz it was slamming on the brakes right in front of me and it did not have working brake lights. It was just THERE! So I veered off to the left to go around it, and just as I was passing the Bug, they turned left right in front of me with no signal, like they were gonna do a U turn or something? The right lower leg of the wide glide smacked right into their left front fender and down the 74 AMF Chopper and me went, metal crunching sounds, scraping on the pavement.

Luckily, I did not flip at first, I just slid along with the bike on its left side on the far left shoulder in the gravel. But then I separated from it and started flipping myself, getting road rash galore. When I finally stopped, I went back to the bike and stood it up looking at the damage. I could see right away a clutch hub stud was busted cuz the derby was all crooked and shit. And all my nice Black Imron Paint and the fresh 4 month old red Doctor Burns Emergency Pin Striping was now gone, cuz the Bug's fender scratched it all off when the lower leg ripped a hole the size of a football in the Bug's fender. So I pushed the bike over to the side out of traffic and parked it, then I was ready to fly into that little bitch and let her have it but good. But instead, a city cop from East Wenatchee pulled right up on the scene. He saw I was ripped up and bloody and he was actually nice to me and asked if I was OK and what had happened. I started telling him the facts, she was speeding, got no license tag, no tail lights, cut me off and hit me. He asked her to turn on her lights,...they didn't work. Hit the brakes,....no brake lights. Her blinkers did not work, so he knew I was telling the truth. And just then, this fuckin' Washington State Patrol goon comes sliding into the scene crunching the gravel under his tires. He jumps outta his car and comes up to the nice cop and me. When I started to explain to the Trooper Pig what was up, he pointed at me and said "You shut up and go wait over by your bike." So I did.

Then as the two teenybopper girls were standing there off to the side, the State Trooper Asshole basically told the nice city cop that this is a state highway and is his turf, to go away, so the nice city cop looked at me, kinda shrugged his shoulders and left. I never saw the trooper asshole ask for the little girl's driver's license. But somehow he knew her name and he kept telling her shit like "Yes, Miss McFarland,....blah blah blah,...I see, Miss McFarland", like she is some kinda little princess or somethin'? So what happened next was the teenybopper's got back into their illegal VW Bug and drove off and I got a ticket from the fuckin' State Trooper prick for "passing within 1,000 feet of an intersection." Can ya believe that shit?

After that pig fucker left, now instead of enjoying a nice ride back out to my camp site, I had to ride the wounded chopper with no working head light and the slipping clutch and busted stud over to Kenny's place, cuz he was the friend I had who lived the closest to where this accident happened. He had just laid me off a few days before, now I'm coming to visit,...uninvited, hah. My ripped and bloody Levis were now trashed, which was a big deal to me cuz I only had 3 pairs to my name, and the road rash was purdy bad, on both knees and legs. And both elbows hurt like hell from smacking the pavement. Oh well, thanks to Friend Kenny the Van Driver, I got a new clutch stud the next day at the combination Harley/Kawasaki dealer and then I put it in at Kenny and Darlene's place out in his cabinet shop.

And then I got really pissed off thinking about that fuckin' ticket. "1,000 feet within an intersection"? That's nearly a 1/4 mile, now who the fuck has a law saying you can't pass within 1/4 of an intersection? So I rode down to the State Patrol head-quarters in downtown Wenatchee to fight this thing. When I walked in, I saw their life size mural on the back wall of 2 State Patrol goons arresting a guy on a chopper. Nice place, eh? So I asked the fuckin' bitch at the desk to look up the number the pig had written on the ticket, cuz I wanna see the law in the books. Of course there was not one, and she made some snide comment about "Looks llike he accidently wrote down the wrong citation number" or some fake lyin' shit like that and told me I'd hafta get a court date to fight it,...so I did. A few days later my court date came up and I went into the courtroom and there he was, the big fat ass prick judge, His Honorable Judge McFarland. So it musta been his grand daughter that nearly killed me? The ticket got thrown out cuz it was a fake ass ticket and the fuckin' State Trooper Pigshitbuttholelicker did not bother to even show up in court,...of course. So, I was set free with no fine.

Now to celebrate this occasion, I rode down to Joe's Log Cabin Tavern to have their delicious fried clam strips and cold Rainier Beer and shoot pool. I stayed til closing time having fun and won a few bucks playin' 8 Ball. And then when every-body was leaving, I walked over and kicked the 74 AMF to life. While I was zipping up my jacket and blabbing to somebody there, out of the corner of my eye I saw the 74 AMF flip its wide glide to the right and like slow motion, it fell over and smacked the curb. Holy shit. And it was a Bull's Eye Hit, cuz the Lectron carb's plastic float bowl hit right on the fuckin' curb, it shattered, and gas was trickling everywhere. So I had to shut off the petcock quick and I gathered up the pieces of the float bowl so

I could show the parts guy what I needed,.....IF,.....they could even find one. I mean, whoever heard of a Lectron carb back then in 1982, and especially in little towns out in the middle of nowhere? I had to push the 74 AMF Chopper over to Reed's house, which was probably a mile and a half, I'd guess, like 15 to 20 blocks or so? And it was an uphill push, cuz it was downhill from Reed's to Joe's Tavern,.....groan.

When I got to Reed's, I didn't wanna wake him up cuz he was a carpet layer and I knew he had to get up in a coupla hours anyhow to go to work. So I parked the chopper in front of his front door and laid down on the ground and tried to sleep. Reed found me the next morning,.....surprise! He gave me the key to his place and took off to work in his 1965 Mustang. I had to walk a mile or so back over to the combination Harley/Kawasaki dealer to order a new Lectron float bowl, which took about a week to come in. So I was stuck being Reed's uninvited house guest for a week or so, while my tent stuff is back out at the river. This picture here is in Reed's back yard. And since I was stuck there waiting for the float bowl to come in, I got some rattle can black and sprayed the right lower leg and thought I might as well do an oil change. Why the fuck not, and that's how May of 1982 went for me. Laid off, hit by a car, paint and new pin stripes fucked up, and carb's float bowl busted.

Chapter 34:

BRIDGE CREEK CAMPGROUND

I settled down and was living in the tent up on Icicle River until I decided to go traveling in the state and see some different country. Why not? All I had to do was be sure I was back in Wenatchee every other week to get the Unemployment Check that was mailed to Reed's place, cash it, and go to the Unemployment Office and fill out another claim the next day or so. This was back when ya had to do that in person.

Paid the rent on the storage unit in Wenatchee and then loaded the tent, sleeping bag, mess kit, and other camping gear on the 74 AMF Chopper, kicked it over and took off up to the North Cascade Highway they also call State Route 20, and went camping up by Wintrop. It was fun riding in perfect cool mountain weather seeing some different sights on new roads that were nice and smooth with no traffic.

But after a few days of heaven, I was missing my old stomping camping grounds so I headed back to the Icicle River, just outside Leavenworth, Washington. I had a good set up there and nobody ever bothered me cuz they didn't have any idea I was there. Don't tell anybody this, but I actually rode through the campground with its official camp sites you are supposed to pay to use, and I rode up onto the foot trail through the woods for maybe 50 yards or so.

I had me a good hidden spot up there that was perfect for the tent and chopper. It was waaay back in the woods, and none of the other campers in the regular camp ground even knew I was in there. Well, they didn't know I was in the back there in the woods until they heard the chopper fire up, then they'd have some funny looks on their mugs when they saw me riding outta the woods on the dirt walking trail coming right at them, This picture here is out there somewhere.

So after the fuckin' stink shit month that May 1982 was, and after I got the Shovel running again with the new plastic float bowl for the Lectron carb, June and July went off really nice, even though the bike was now without its fancy red pin stripes on the right lower leg,...sniff, sniff. It was the shits how the nice upgrade on the 74 Chopper I had done back in Dallas in January didn't even make it a full 4 months, but that's the way it goes for a Homeless Chopper Hobo, eh?

Now I am gonna try to take you inside my main campground home. Too bad I didn't have a video camera back then cuz the sights of the mountains at the campground and the sounds of the crashing Icicle River woulda been hella-cool to see and listen to on video. So the best we can do is look at the pictures and use our imaginations, ha-ha-ha.

Icicle River is outside the little Bavarian town of Leavenworth, right in the center of Washington State. I have never been to Europe cuz there ain't roads and bridges long enough to ride there, but people tell me that Leavenworth is like being in the Swiss Alps. Snowcapped mountains stick straight up to the sky in town, and the town itself is all old timey German architecture, little buildings with flower baskets handing over the covered sidewalks, stuff like that. And in the winter time it really snows tons there, they even had one of those big ass ski jumps built back in the 1930s for the Olympic Athletes to practice on, the kind where you go down the jump doing 60 mph and then go zinging out into the air, like Wide World of Sports, Agony of Defeat. Anyhow, this is supposed to be about bikes, not the skiers. I'm just trying to let ya know it was very mountainous territory.

So from the Main Drag in Leavenworth, I'd ride out to the edge of town and turn left to go up Icicle River Road. You ride along next to the crashing river on your left side, with rock walls on your right side and the upsweep fish tail pipes echoing off the rocks. All around you is huge mountains. You keep riding for maybe 20 minutes, all gradual uphill ride, following the curves of the Icicle River. When you get to Bridge Creek Campground, you turn left onto the dirt road. That's where this picture was taken. From the dirt road, you can go to the right and cross over the bridge over the Icicle River. But that is not where I camped. I turned off to the left and followed the river. On the right-hand side of this dirt road there is maybe 8 to 10 campsites, with permanent rock firepits to have your camp fires. On the left side,...umm,...maybe just 4 or 5 campsites, and on that side is a well with a pump for water, even though I just drank the Icicle River and lived to tell about it cuz it's fresh water, hahaha, and there is a for real outhouse on the left side. And I don't mean one of those fake Porta Johns, I mean a for real stink ass outhouse, where you just bomb away, see? It stunk like shit. I always wondered why, hah.

I'd keep riding to the left side of the campground until I got to the end, the last Official Camp Site there was. Oh, and this was an Honor System camp ground where they had the big wooden box for you to drop money in the slot for your tent spot. And yes, I always paid, cuz it was the least I could do, since I didn't have a house payment or rent to come up with, hahaha. But that ain't where I camped, either. I'd keep on ridin' the chopper right through the campground and keep on going where ya ain't supposed to go, right up the little 3-foot-wide hiking trail maybe 50 yards or so. To the left on the trail was a nice flat spot in the pine trees with soft needles for the tent to go on. There were plenty of trees to lean the chopper up against, cuz the kickstand would sink in the needles. And yes, I tried putting a flat rock under the kickstand and that didn't work either, the bike was on its side on the ground the next morning, hah. So I'd set up the tent, lean the chopper up against a tree, and I had a little creek maybe 3 or 4 feet wide that was my fridge. I'd put my eggs, meat, beer, juice, apples, whatever needed to go into a fridge would go into the creek. I trapped water with rocks the size of bowling balls and made a little circular pool to put my stuff in. I'd also wrap my food in plastic bags and sink it to the bottom with rocks cuz there were black bears in the area.

In the mornings, the first thing I'd wake up to was the sound of crashing white water splashing over the boulders in the river. I'd start the camp fire and get breakfast going. I could do bacon and eggs, camp fire toast, or ham and eggs, oatmeal, just about whatever you can cook at home I could cook out there. After I ate, I'd wait until the sun came up over the mountains, which could be around 10:00 AM or so, cuz it gets light there kinda early but you don't see the actual sun come up until it gets over the ridge, see? And then once the sun hit, it would get warm and I could jump in the river to get clean. I had a spot that was like a swimming pool with calm water, right next to the crashing water. It was like taking a bath in 33 degrees Champagne with all the bubbles coming up, hahaha. And there was a big tree about 3 feet in diameter that had fallen down years earlier I'm guessing, and it laid across the boulders. So I used that tree to dry my clothes on. I'd wash them in the river, then squeeze 'em dry, then lay 'em out across the tree trunk with rocks on them the size of grapefruits to keep 'em from blowing away. And that is how I lived out in the woods.

After I'd do the clothes and wash my breakfast dishes and mess kit, then I'd kick the chopper over and ride into Leavenworth. It was one of the most fun rides ever, going into that town. They had a little German bakery, grocery store, little auto parts store, hardware and likker store, gas station, whatever you needed, they seemed to have it. There was a Billiard Palace there, too. It was called The Ratzkeller and was run by a little Austrian guy named Waldo. Him and me used to shoot pool and play snooker all the time. I could eat lunch in town if I wanted, grab a burger or sammich, then go get the groceries for camp fire supper that night. Looking back now, it was the most peaceful and tranquil time of my life. I had nothing to worry about, except keeping the bike in top shape and the fuckin' Washington State Patrol Pigshit Asswipes, especially Officer Truman Douglas the most rotten-ist pigshit of them all. Oh yeah, and as you can see on the bike, I'm still running the Texas license tag, which pissed off them troopers to no end. Good.

Living in the woods had two different types of things happen. There was the Rich Version and the Poor Version. The Rich Version was when the Unemployment Check would come in and I'd cash it at Joe's Log Cabin Tavern on the edge of Wenatchee, one of my main hangouts back then. I got 163 bucks a week, which meant the 2 week check would be 326 bucks, and no rent or bills to pay. So on those first days after getting the check cashed, I'd be filthy rich. I'd get a T Bone Steak, corn on the cob, and a tater for baking. I'd get a good camp fire going, wrap the tater in aluminum foil and stick in down under the hot coals and let it go for an hour or so. Up on top of the fire, I'd do the steak and corn on my little fold out camping grill. Cold frosty Rainier Beer was over in the creek about 10 feet away, so I'd hafta mosey all the way over there to get it, bwahahaha.

I could cook burgers, pork chops, whatever else I felt like eating while I was rich. But then? A few days before the next check came in, I'd be a poor sumbitch. And for those nights supper would be a can of chili in the fire, or a can of beans heated up, or maybe hot dogs or the ol' faithful peanut butter and jelly sammitches. And that's the way life was for me in the woods.

And here's where I kept the chopper parked, right in front of my front tent door. And that is my little creek over behind the chopper.

Living in the woods didn't mean I was always alone. I'd have visitors come by, sometimes people, sometimes animals, ha ha-ha. Jim that I worked with had his black 75 Sportster and he'd ride out from Wenatchee to visit and smoke weed and drink beer. Kenny my carpenter boss had a big Yamaha and he'd drop by once in a while, too. And then there were the other people from other towns that would stop in the campground to camp for the weekend. Those folks kinda ticked me off at times. Ya see, firewood was not all that plentiful in the campground back then. I had to scrounge for it. And these city folks would show up and they'd build big ass fires and burn up enough fire wood in one night that I coulda cooked on for a fuckin' week.... but on the flip side, sometimes when they'd leave the camp Sunday afternoon to go back to work, they'd sometimes leave maybe a half bag of charcoal, or maybe an old pot or skillet or some fire wood sticks. I'd scrounge that stuff, too. I was a true hobo hermit & recycler, hah.

I also had little stashes of things I'd hide around the area. My main hiding spot for wood was down in the rocks by the water. Who'd go to the water to look for dry wood, right? There'd be natural little caves in the rocks and I could stash things in them and place rocks in front and nobody ever knew anything was in there.

There were also days it rained like crazy and that was when it was toughest to find dry firewood to cook with, see? So that's why all that shit was so important to me.

If I had cash and it rained, no biggie, I'd ride in the drizzly rain into Leavenworth and eat at one of the joints there. But there were also times it rained and I was broke, so I'd just sit in the tent and watch it rain. Kinda boring, but also relaxing, that is, as long as I didn't accidently touch the tent. Do ya know what happens when you touch the top of a tent while it's raining? It starts leaking on you at the spot where you touched it, bwahaha. So if I even accidently touched the top of the tent with my elbow, then I had to move the sleeping bag to keep it from getting wet. This hobo stuff can get really tricky and corn-fusin' at times, eh? This picture here looks like it was one of the poor nights, we're havin' a can of beans for supper. Yummy, eh? And lookie there at that nice firewood stash! I was set for a few days now.

Chapter 35:

THE BILLIARD HUSTLE

A fun thing happened in the beginning of July 1982 for me. I was in downtown Leavenworth shootin' pool at the Ratzkeller, the billiard hall the Austrian guy Walter owned. There were a few guys in there and we were shootin' 8 Ball,.....2 bucks a game. I was up by maybe 16 or 18 bucks,.....big money for an unemployed Chopper Hobo like me back then. After I beat the last guy, he got kinda pissy, said I was the luckiest guy he ever saw shootin' 8 Ball. I didn't have the heart to tell him I was a Regulation 8 Ball Champion in Dallas back in 1971, got in the newspaper and got to meet Willie Mosconi, but that's another story for another time, hahaha.

So the ticked off dude yanks his wallet out, pulls out a 20 dollar bill, smacks it down on the pool table and sez "I've got 20 bucks here if you wanna take me on in a Call Shot game to 50 points. Do you even know how to play Call Shot?" He said it just like that, kinda semi-insulting. Hmm,.....if there was one thing I was better at than 8 Ball, it was Call Shot, otherwise known as 14.1 Continuous Billiards. So I sez back to the guy, "You mean Call Shot, where we shoot any ball we want to as long as we call it?" He said yes, so it was Game On.

We lagged for break, I won, so I told him to break. He did. Long story short, I ran up my 50 points and won the game with everyone watching while he was still around 22 points, so I won his 20 dollar bill. Now what would a 27 year old unemployed punk kid Chopper Hobo do with a new freebie 20 dollar bill? Buy some oil for the chopper? Nope, just did the oil change at Reed's place while the Lectron float bowl was busted. Buy some gas or beer with the free 20? Nope, that is normal stuff, it wouldn't be that much fun.

What I did I still remember to this day. I walked outta the Ratzkeller billiard palace and moseyed over to the fanciest German restaurant in town, Katzenjammers. I went in there and plopped my tent livin' unemployed chopper pilot butt down at a table and I had Alaskan King Crab Legs! First time in my life I ever ate them. I don't have any idea how many of you folks ever saw Alaskan King Crabs, but them suckers can grow up to 6 feet across. And that means the legs I had on my platter in front of me were maybe 18 to 24 inches long, ha-ha ha! They split them suckers with a little saw and I dug out the crab meat with a little fork and had them with melted butter. They were fantastic....and free for me. Washed 'em down with Vitamin R..... Rainier Beer.

This picture here is my automatic solar clothes dryer, a big tree trunk log across the Icicle River where I'd put the rocks on the clothes to keep 'em from blowing away.

OK now I'm gonna try somethin' on here I've never done before. I did not have any video back in 1982, of course, but I did do this time lapse picture thing-a-ma-bob. I was out on the trails walking around,...gotta have something free to do when you're a Chopper Hobo, right? And while I was up on the side of the mountain, I heard this really loud SMACK! CRASH! sound, like a city bus running into a brick wall. I was like what the fuck is that noisy shit waaaay out here in the middle of nowhere? Then

I looked up and I saw the entire side of the mountain in front of me collapse down into the lake...... Landslide!

Since I had the camera with me, I took a picture of it maybe every 5 seconds or so. Some are vertical some are horizontal. And they've been in the old photo albums for soooo long now that they are stuck, I could not pull 'em out to scan them. So, I took a picture of the pictures. I'll post them here in order so you can see what happened. I don't think anybody ever knew about this except for me and the animals...

After the month of May sucking ass with the little teenybopper running me down with her illegal bird shit spattered muddy VW Bug fresh outta the junkyard with the fucking State Patrol goon giving me the ticket for the wreck she caused, and with the 74 AMF Chopper falling over while I was drunk and busting its float bowl on the curb and leaving me stuck in Wenatchee for a week waiting for another one to come in the mail, June was a purdy nice month and July was shaping up to be a nice one, too.

Next I had some visitors come out to visit. No, it wasn't black bears or Bigfoot, it was Scott that I had worked with in the cabinet shop & his wife Bonnie, their daughter Vanessa and their pal Jim, who always had good weed. We had fun smoking and drinking around the campfire that evening and making supper and breakfast the next day. Here's some pictures of the action and the little creek that was my free fridge. You can see the eggs down in the water and some Miller Beers floating around.

Previously, I posted the photos of the 74 AMF Chopper leaning up against the tree and the picture of my Home Sweet Home, aka The Green & Yeller Tent. Now here's some photos looking the other way, from the tent area out. This is the first thing I saw and heard every morning and the last thing I saw and heard at night,...my swimmin' hole where I'd get clean in melted snow water that made my balls shrink up to my tonsils, bwahaha. They don't call it the Icicle River fer nuthin', see? And there is one really tricky picture in here in this mess of 'em. I set the timer on the Canon AE-1 camera for 10 seconds, then ran out there over the fuckin' rocks and climbed up on the tree trunk/clothes dryer and risked my pathetic Chopper Hobo life taking this crummy picture just so's you could laugh at it 39 years later.

OK here's 5 more shots of Icicle River, the area in Central Washington where I was chopper living in the tent. I'm loading up these photos cuz we gotta be movin' on soon, cuz it's about time we rode the 74 AMF Chopper down to California for a good paying job, something I ain't had in 2 years in Dallas, hah aha ha....

Here is some more Chopper Hobo Experimental Photography from the camp site area in Central Washington where I lived in the tent. These mountains were too huge to get all in one shot. So I steadied the camera up against a tree trunk with the camera in the vertical position. I paid attention to where the cross hairs lined up on the mountain, then snapped the photo. Then I moved the camera over to where the left side of the next shot lined up with the trees on the right side of the previous shot, took the photo, then moved it over one more time for the far right side shot. When I got them developed, I took all 3 photos and slid them together in the photo album to make this big ass picture. They give those Hollywood dorks prestigious awards for doing less work than this, bwahaha. Here it is for you, for free, three shots into one.

Here is another shot of some of the high ridges where I was still living in the tent in the Cascades.

Chapter 36:

GOODBYE WENATCHEE

By the middle of July,... I could sadly see the writing on the wall. I would soon hafta leave this Chopper Hobo Paradise I had accidently stumbled into and go back to the real working world. Sigh.

These are some of the last shots I took of my tent home. And Kim Kardashian thinks she invented selfies? I'm doin' 'em right here in 1982, setting the timer on the camera and running over to the tent to get into the picture. I'd take selfie pictures like this and mail them back to Dallas like a post card just to let them all know I was still kickin',.....barely. Another photo in this group is what I think is a lava forest, where the trees on top grew outta ancient old lava spews. I could be wrong, but that's what it looked like to me. The little bare area photo with the rocks was my 'front yard' in front of the tent, and what a crooked zig zag tree trunk, eh?

OK, now for the bad part. During the past 12 months I had been on unemployment in Washington State since back in the fall of 1981, then I had worked in Dallas for 3 months, then got laid off, rode back up to Washington, worked 2 months, got laid off again and had to do one of those Interstate Unemployment claims that gets nice and complicated. In other words, I didn't have a whole lotta unemployment money left in that account and I needed to find a job somewhere before that claim ran out and winter set in. I did not wanna be unemployed and broke in Washington in the winter time. That would suck big time. It was decision time.

So next I rode the chopper over to Wenatchee to the little storage unit I had rented and I dug into my old bag of phone numbers and pulled out the number for a guy named Pete who was a traveling Construction Superintendent that I had worked for in Dallas a few years earlier. Pete's company was called Columbia Showcase and they specialized in doing the woodwork in fancy high end department stores, like Neiman Marcus, Sak's Fifth Avenue, Lord & Taylor, fancy shit like that. It was good inside work. So I called up ol' Pete and told him I am stuck up in Washington State and need a job. I said I was willing to travel anywhere on the west coast, from San Diego up to Vancouver British Columbia. Pete said he was working on a brand-new

Neiman Marcus store right then in San Francisco and I could come on down whenever I wanted to, he'd have a job waiting for me. BINGO! Major score for me.

I told him I could be there in 4 days. That would give me a day to get my shit together at the camp site and go through the storage unit, and a day that Kenny would let me build up a 2X4 and plywood crate in his shop in order to ship my carpenter tool box down to San Francisco. Then that would leave me 2 days to make the 800-mile chopper ride. So I did it. Got the crate made and a trucking guy in an 18-wheeler came by Kenny's shop and loaded up my tool box. He was gonna haul it down to San Francisco for 50 bucks. I was very happy he'd do it. And then after we loaded the crate on and the guy drove off, I panicked, bwahahaha! What if I never saw my toolbox again? How would I make a living?

Next I loaded up the chopper with the road bag, a few clothes and the tent and sleeping bag, cuz who knows where I'll be sleeping next,...right?

I must admit, although I've done it several times now in 4 different states, every time I ride the chopper away to start a new segment of life, it kinda scares the shit outta me for a little bit, and this time was maybe one of the worst? Cuz I had no idea where my toolbox was, just hoped that it was making its way to San Francisco on the 18 wheeler driven by a total stranger, hah. At this point in my life, besides the 74 AMF Chopper, the toolbox was the most important thing to me, cuz without it, I ain't got no tools and can't earn a living.

Anyhow, I said goodbye to all the nice folks in Wenatchee, paid the rent on the storage unit for the next 6 months and took off on the chopper. I still had a lot of nice mountainous high country to ride through.

Here's a road side shot on the way down to California, going from tent living in the Washington Cascades. This was out east of Ellensburg and I stopped here to take a stretch and smoke some devil weed. Around a half day's ride comes the Oregon border, the big ass Columbia River.

Sidenote: Do you folks realize how much the name "Columbia" has come into play in this saga, hahaha? The little cabinet shop I had been working at was called Columbia Woodwork, and it was on Columbia Street on the bank of the Columbia River. And now I am riding the chopper off to San Francisco to go to work for a huge company from Los Angeles called,... what else? Columbia Showcase.

OK so the rent was paid up for 6 months on the storage unit in Wenatchee, the toolbox was shipped on a semi truck down to San Francisco, the 74 AMF Chopper was packed with the road gear and we took off headed to San Francisco for a job-bie-job working on building a new Neiman Marcus store for the rich folks to shop at. Oooh la la. Now it's time to leave Wenatchee,...again.

The chopper was fulla gas and running just fine in the clean mountain air as I rode over Blewett Pass on Highway 97 headed to Ellensburg, one of the nicest rides you can imagine. The weather was perfect. When I got to Ellensburg, I wanted to stop in and visit my riding buddies, but didn't have time, cuz I gotta be in San Francisco in two days and it's a little over 800 miles away. So at Ellensburg, I took I-82 through Yakima by 14,411 feet high Mount Rainier on down to Toppenish. From there, I switched back over to Highway 97 and kept riding on the smaller road headed toward The Dalles, Oregon. I crossed the big ass Columbia River at the border and continued on west, headed toward Portland now on I-84. When I got by Portland I turned south and caught the old stand by, I-5, one of the main arteries on the west coast for hauling ass north and south.

From there is was a piece of cake as for switching highways, cuz I-5 is gonna get me purdy damn close to where I wanna go. I rode through Salem, Corvallis, Eugene, on down to Roseburg. That was nearly a 500 mile ride that day and took me all damn day to do it, stopping only for gas, eats, and weed breaks. I got a cheapie roadside motel room for the night.

This picture here is the big volcano bump known as Mount Rainier, and this may be the barest picture of it that I have, cuz it usually had more snow on it. Musta been a dry year for them back then.

I ended up spending the night at a roadside motel in Roseburg, Oregon, on I-5 which was about half way for the trip from Wenatchee Washington to San Francisco. Woke up, showered,.....which was a nice change from jumping in the Icicle River like I had been doing, ha ha-ha,.....ate a breakfast that somebody else cooked for me, which was also a nice change from my campfire vittels, and then I gassed up the 74 AMF Contraption and headed on down the road, south on I-5 headed to Californy.

I-5 took me through Grants Pass, then on to Medford and Ashland. I was getting closer to the state line and the weather was perfect for a road trip, nice and sunny. I crossed the California state line and rode through Yreka and on down to the town of Mount Shasta, which is kinda close to Mount Shasta, hahaha. Strange, eh? Kept riding through the mountains to Redding, then the landscape kinda flattened out a bit, kept on riding to Red Bluff and then Willows.

Kept heading toward Sacramento, but before I got there, turned off on I-505 headed to Vacaville which is on I-80. From there I took the smaller highways to Vallejo cuz I was wanting to catch Highway 101 since I wanted to ride the chopper into San Francisco crossing the Golden Gate Bridge, not through the Oakland area. And around sunset I had finally made it into San Francisco. So now what?

Don't know a soul in the entire state except for Pete my old boss from Dallas and I ain't seen him yet. So I rode on into the downtown part of Frisco and got me a nice cheap shabby ass room in a scummy flea bag 5 story hotel called the Civic Center Hotel, and this is it right here. Ain't it a classy joint? The guy at the front desk was from India and he wore a big turban on his noggin, and he worked from behind 1-inch-thick bullet proof glass. How quaint. He gave me a room up on the 3rd floor and I chained up the 74 AMF Shovel to the No Parking sign on the sidewalk in front of the hotel. So I guess this is my new home? Yikes, ha ha-ha. And just a few nights before I was living in the tent on the Icicle River all nice and calm, and now here I am in the scummy part of SF.

Chapter 37:

SAN FRANCISCO

A rriving into San Francisco at sunset on Sunday August 1, 1982, and getting a filthy room in the cockroach flea bag known as the Civic Center Hotel in the scummy part of downtown Frisco on Market close to Van Ness. I jumped up outta the crummy bed that had those lousy buttons sewn into the cheap ass mattress, the kind of buttons that poke you in the back and keep you awake all damn night. Hell the sleeping bag in the tent was better than this flea bag hotel shit. Now lemme tell ya about this hotel and my room up on the 3rd floor. Where do I start?

First, the red carpet was barely red anymore cuz of all the filth, and remember, I had been used to living in DIRT on the river, bwah a ha-ha! The yellowed ceiling had the paint peeling off, and it was 10 feet up to it. There was a bare light bulb that hung down and you pulled one of those little chains made out of the metal balls, if you folks are old enough to remember that funny shit. I had a crappy bed, a tiny little sink mounted on the wall,... and,.............. and that was it. No bathroom, no closet, no kitchen area, no nuthin'. The road side motels were nicer than this shitty joint. All the rooms were like that. We had a long stinky nasty hallway on the floor and we all shared one bathroom.

So I jumped in the shower early that Monday morning before the junkies, winos, hookers, pimps, and other assorted vagrants woke up. I got into the shower first, cuz I found out later if you waited too long, the bathroom would be covered in puke. I found that out the hard way. Not good.

After the semi-hot shower and getting dressed, I hoofed it down to the chopper on the sidewalk still chained up to the No Parking sign. Good. At least it was still there, I kicked it over and took off for Union Square, and the gal at the front desk that worked days told me how to get there,.....just go straight down Market Street til ya get to Stockton, turn left and go 2 blocks up to Geary and there ya are, smack dab in the middle of Union Square. It was an easy ride, didn't even take 5 minutes.

I pulled the chopper up inside the fence that went around the construction site, went in and saw Pete the Superintendent, the guy that I had worked for in Dallas back in 1978. I had to pull off an act this time, though. Ya see, Pete remembered me as the young enterprising whippersnapper, 23 years old with his own house, a fancy chopper, custom built Corvette, and lots of work connections. Now I was a homeless hobo, no house, no car, no nuthin' except for the chopper and the toolbox. And that tool box was sitting right there inside the jobsite where Pete had the guys unload it and put it in their lockup room. It was good to see the toolbox had made it unharmed, thanks to the nice tough crate I was able to make for it at Kenny's shop back up in Wenatchee.

I checked in with Pete and he said for me to start the next day, to go get my stuff together. I didn't really have any stuff to get together, ha-ha ha. They gave me a hard hat and I walked around the job site checking it out. I heard all kinds of foreign languages being spoken, cuz the majority of the crew were Europeans. German, French, Italian, Japanese, English, Irish, Scots, Sicilians, you name it. Later I found out the foreman named Mac was a retired Air Force Colonel from Amarillo Texas and there was a guy named Ed that was from Kansas. I think we were the only ones there that were born in the USA, ha ha-ha. OK I have been blabbing about the Koa Wood toolbox I made, so here it is.

I got situated at the job site and went to work, Yawn….. Well the first thing that happened to me was the entire crew laughing at me cuz of my Lee coveralls. Ya see, in Dallas all the carpenters wore Lee coveralls with the blue and white stripes. I wore them up in Washington, too. So that's what I was wearing. But in San Francisco, all the carpenters wore white Ben Davis coveralls. So when the main guys on the crew saw me, they laughed and said "So what the fuck are you? A gawddamn train engineer, hahaha?" And that's how it went, hah. So I had to tough it out for a coupla weeks until I got a pay check and got some white ones. Big deal, I got over it. I made fun of their metal and plastic toolboxes so we were even, wink, wink.

So what about the social life? Well, since you asked, here goes, hahaha. A few days after I got into Frisco, I discovered the flea bag hotel was actually kind of a cool place to live, as far as the location was. Ya see, I had Frisco Choppers a coupla blocks to the south of me on Valencia, and Dudley Perkins HD Dealer,…the oldest one in the world since 1914,… was a coupla blocks north of me on Page Street. (Both shops are now gone.)

Haight Street also ends by where I was, but not the cool fun hippie part of Haight, it's the Lower Haight, which was the Ghetto Haight back then. After I had been in Frisco for a few days, one day I was eating at a little grocery store on Haight Street at FIllmore. I met this gal there named Judy. We were talking and she asked me if I wanted to get high. I said I was already high, hardy har har.

She suggested we go around the corner to her place, so we did. She lived in sort of an abandoned art gallery, maybe from the 1930s, on its last legs. She had electricity in the place, but no running water, cuz she was behind on the water bill and they had shut her water off. She had crazy paintings hanging on the walls, some pottery stuff, and a coupla sculptures with a killer big stereo system hooked up. We smoked some weed, drank some Champagne she had in her fridge that was nice and cold, and after a coupla more days, next thing ya know, she invited me to move in there with her.

So I did. What won me over was when she said "Hey, as far as I am concerned your chopper is high class art. You should move it inside here so it is safe." How could you resist an invitation like that? So my new borrowed temporary address was at 551 Haight Street and here it is, with the chopper parked out on the sidewalk this time.

I grabbed my bag from the flea bag hotel and moved into 551 Haight Street with Judy. When I got the next paycheck I rode downtown and paid up her delinquent water bill so she had running water again,...yay. I had joined a gym close by and took showers there, while Judy had been using her neighbor's bathroom for a while, hah. She had weed and Champagne, but couldn't keep the water running?

And here is one really weird thing about where she lived, and the three neighbors on each side of her had the same set up. You walked into the place, ultra high ceiling, like 20 feet up there, and they were long skinny rooms with kitchens in the back. For sleeping, you walked back toward the front, but instead of going out the front door, there were ladders you climbed up to sleep in the loft overlooking the sidewalk out front.

But wait, there's more. There ain't no bathrooms inside the places that's right, you had to walk out the back door and out there was a big wooden deck that connected all the units, an old semi rotten deck, and the toilet and shower were out there in a little room on the deck. It blew me away. I asked Judy "Why in the hell is the bathroom outside? Don't those pipes ever freeze up on you?" She just gave me her Natasha from Rocky and Bullwinkle smile and said "Dave. It never gets that cold here. The weather is always nice." Hmm. Well, what will they think of next?

Then next up the block for social life is my new riding partner. Check this out. Sunday in late August I was at a bar in the Upper Haight kinda close to Golden Gate Park. I had been in there for an hour or so, shootin' pool and playin' the juke box, when I decided to leave. I walked out to the chopper on the curb, turned on the gas, flipped the toggle switch for 'on' and I kicked it over. Fired up good and I swung a leg over, pushed in the foot clutch and stuck the shifter stick back into 1st gear, got ready to take off when this maroon Shovel comes blasting around the corner, spies me sitting there, slams on his brakes and backs in next to me and shuts off his motor.

He sez "Far out man, that is one cool chopper!" I said thanks. I also wondered who sez 'far out' anymore? He got off and started walking around the Shovel, checking it out. When he got to the back end, he spotted the Texas license tag. He sez, "You from Texas?" I said yep, he sez "What part?" I said Dallas, then he said he was from Texas, raised in San Marcos. I told him "I love San Marcos and used to go ride the big inner tubes down the river there." I told him my name was Dave, he said his was Steve. So he said come on in and I'll buy you a beer."

We grabbed a coupla stools at the bar and started bullshittin' and it seemed like we were twins separated at birth. Within maybe 15 minutes we found out we were both born in Texas, born the same year 1955, born the same month and I was 3 days older than him, and both sets of our parents hated motorcycles and we both left the folks' houses over getting bikes, ha-ha ha.

We had a few nice cold frosty beers and then Steve ordered us two shots of Jose, with limes and salt. We did the shots. When Steve smacked his shot glass down on the bar, he turned toward me with a dead pan face, no expression, stuck his thumb under his armpit and flapped it up and down like a chicken and yelled out really loud "GUAWW! NEET! NEET! NEET! PFFFT! PFFFT! PFFFT! GAHHH... INDIANS!" And he kept looking at me with that wry smile Jack Nicholson did and I nearly fell off my bar stool laughing at how fuckin' funny he was. It was a perfect imitation. I knew that very second that I had found a new riding partner and a really funny new friend, and all just a coincidence that we even met. Out on the curb before, I already had the chopper in gear and was ready to pull out from the curb. If Steve had been 30 seconds later, we woulda never met and my life woulda taken a totally different turn. It was destiny, hah.

Later we rode up on top of the highest hill in Frisco called Twin Peaks and smoked a joint I had with me in the handlebars, and back then you could actually ride up to the top, they hadn't turned it into the tourist trap yet, it was just a bare big hill. Here's the photo from it. Once again, I set the Canon camera down on a rock, set the timer for 10 seconds and ran over to the chopper for the picture. Steve just stood there like I was nuts.

Chapter 38:

OAKLAND, SAN FRANCISCO.

On the job front things were going well, the boss man teamed me up with an older Japanese carpenter named Kuro Saki who was a woodworking genius. We were the two guys who did all the woodwork in The Rotunda, which was a vaulted stained-glass ceiling 7 floors up in the air. The Rotunda had originally been in the center of the previous historical City of Paris Building which had been demoed. The glass had been carefully disassembled, sent to a shop where they spent 2 million bucks restoring it. The entire thing was shipped back to this new building where it was used for the main entrance. So if anyone reading this ever walks into that Neimans store on Union Square, you can step inside the main entrance, look 7 floors up to the ceiling, and now you know one of the two guys who did that all that woodwork. It took us about 10 weeks to do it.

Now you guys can see why it took us a few weeks to do it, hahaha. And that photo is shot from the inside part of The Rotunda Restaurant. Where the camera was, there are radiused booths and tables for eating vittels. Behind where the camera was is the kitchen area.

In 1987 on a summer Saturday afternoon, we were eating lunch there with my sister-in-law who was visiting us on vacation from Milwaukee. While we were eating, I looked up and saw Mister Kuro Saki walking around the Rotunda feeling the joints in the top of the handrail, checking out our work, maybe to see if the little earthquakes had damaged it? I jumped up and walked over to him and had him join us for lunch. This was just before he sold his house in San Francisco and moved back to Tokyo. And then the big quake came in October of 1989. -Trivia

Meanwhile on the Motorcycle Front, Steve introduced me to Oakland, where he lived. And here's how he did it. We were in a bar on Haight and the subject of the Oakland Bay Bridge came up. I was dumb, didn't know a damn thing about it yet, ha-ha ha. I told Steve I had ridden over the Golden Gate a coupla times, but never the Oakland Bay Bridge. So he gulped his beer down and said "C'mon, you've got no idea what you've been missing out on."

We fired up the two Shovels and took off down Oak Street, which is one way and set up to hit the green lights good when you are headed east on it. We got to the spot where we hit the ramp to get up on the highway and rolled the throttles on. We mixed in with the car traffic and got in the center lane. I was following Steve's lead. That bridge went up and up, next thing we were up really high, looking out at the Bay, ships going underneath us with the mountains in the background. After we crested the top, then we started down and I found out what is so great about that bridge.....it's 8 & 1/2 miles long and has a fantastic fuckin' tunnel going through Treasure Island, bwahaha!

We wracked the pipes off really good inside there, and then we shot out the other end and went over the second half of the bridge. When it landed in Oakland above the piers, we got off at an early ramp cuz that was Steve's exit. Lake Merritt was there and the wonderful old timey Paramount Theater. We rode up the main drag kinda slow, then turned right after the theater, then turned left and there we were at his place. And now I finally understood how Oakland places are cheaper rents and they ain't that far away to get to. Steve's apartment building was an old one, probably 1930s, two floors, 8 units. No garage in the back, but they did have covered car ports. Like me, Steve didn't own a car either so he didn't hafta worry about where to park one.

As for the Home Life Front,....umm. They say a gentleman never kisses and tells. But I do. At 551 Haight Street, I wound up with the crabs, and not the Alaska King Crabs kind. Yep, after paying the late water bills and getting it turned back on in the place, I got the favor returned by a nice mess of crabs. I was itchy like crazy at work, ha-ha ha. I had no idea what the crabs were until this older guy at work told me.

When he was telling me, I still didn't get it, then he started saying it's like lice, or ringworm, and then it freaked me out, after work that day I went to a store and got some Qwell 200 and all new clothes, Levis, shirt, socks and BVDs. I rode over to Japan Town to the Kabuki Baths and rented a room and deloused myself with that Qwell 200 stuff. I showered multiple times, hah, cuz the guy at work had really put the fear in me. Then I threw all my old clothes in the bag and left them in the corner of the room for somebody else to enjoy.

Then I rode back to Judy's place at 551, got my stuff from there, said a polite but quick goodbye, rode to the coin op laundry up the street on Haight and cleaned everything as good as I could, ha ha-ha. And then I rode back over to the Civic Center Hotel and got another room there. It may have been a dump, but at least I didn't get crabs there. And that's how September 1982 went for me. Here's the only picture I got of Judy, dammit. We were trying to get to Ocean Beach for a nice sunset picture, but we got there too late.

So this is what we wound up with. Judy and the chopper's headlight.

Chapter 39:

No Brakes

October was a good month, with Steve showing me the East Bay area, he took me to his favorite bars and the East Bay bike shops, We rode to Bob Dron's HD dealer. Then we rode over to one of the main drags called Foothill Blvd and went by a head shop called Puff & Stuff, which I think is one of the oldest head shops in Oakland, and it was right next to the Angels Club House, then we rode on down south on Foothill until we got to Hayward and we stopped in at Ron Simms Bay Area Custom Cycle. I wish to hell I had the camera with me this day but I didn't.

From BACC we rode back up and over to San Leandro to Arlen's shop. This was my favorite stop of the day. When we walked in the front door, Arlen had his parts counter on the left-hand side and a glass wall on the right-hand side of his shop and there were all his latest Bay Area Digger Style masterpieces lined up against that glass wall, the ones I had seen in the magazines, including his Knuckle he had Swiss Cheesed, the one he drilled all the holes in. I got a T shirt from his shop and still have it today.

From there we rode back up to Berkeley and hit Telegraph Avenue and rode over by an old Triumph shop there and then hit the big 2 story coffee house there on the street. I got introduced to Italian coffee that day, drawn straight out of the big ass brass and copper espresso machines by hand, not the automatic crap they do today in the 'coffee boutiques' This was real coffee served in real coffee houses the beatniks used, coffee houses the likes of which my Dallas born ass had never seen or even heard of.

Then we rode up Mount Diablo, not a big ass mountain by Rocky or Cascade Mountain standards, but around 4,000 feet and I think it's the highest peak in the Bay Area, more than 1,000 feet higher than Mount Tam on the north side of the Bay Area. And then it was time to get high again and go have some drinks. Here's ya a semi-stormy lookin' photo of some Bay Area salt water with the Golden Gate Bridge in the background.

Sunday Halloween weekend 1982 in the Bay Area was one of the scariest but funniest yet cheapest and easiest breakdowns I ever had. I had been hanging out in Oakland all day with Steve riding our Shovels around the East Bay. But it was now getting to be Sunday evening and I had to go to work the next day so I headed back to Frisco across the Oakland Bay Bridge. Riding outta Frisco on either bridge was always free, but they had a toll to get back in.

So, I'm riding along on the chopper not a care in the world, coming up to the toll booth to get back in. I down shifted from 4th to 3rd, wracked the pipes off some, then hit the back brake coming up to the toll booth, only to discover I ain't got no back brake, bwah ah aha! Nuthin'! I quickly shifted down to 2nd and hit the front brake, but my front brake was a Panhead drum and any of you who run those old things knows how 'great' they work, ha ha-ha. I guided the chopper in between the moving cars and worked my way over to the far-right side lane. Then I got down into 1st gear and started dragging my boots to stop, in a semi-panic. I finally stopped over on the right-hand side by the guard rail. Whew!

Now to see what the fuck happened? I shut the motor off and leaned it over on the kick stand. Walked around to the right side to look at the brake pedal. It was still hooked up. But where it went into the cross over tube......the clevis pin was gone, so that means the cotter came out and then the pin went. Fuck. Now what the hell am I gonna do? Standing there looking at the ground, among the broken glass, plastic shit garbage, paper bags and old smashed beer cans I spied one of those gigantic big ass paper clips. I straightened out the paper clip and wound it around and through the hole connecting it back to the cross over piece. Bingo. It worked perfect.

I kicked the chopper over, got back in line, paid the toll, and rode on back to the flea bag Civic Center Hotel. The next day after work I rode over to Frisco Choppers and got the right parts. This here is another picture of Steve and our two Shovels up on Twin Peaks again where we puffed a lot. And no, it ain't the same picture as before cuz I ain't in it and he's got on different clothes.

Chapter 40:

MAKING THE LAYOFF LIST.

Steve on his Shovelhead was showing me the hot spots of the East Bay, riding down Foothill Blvd to the Puff & Stuff head shop by the Angels club house, on down to Hayward to Ron Simms Bay Area Custom Cycle, then back up to San Leandro to Arlen's shop where I got a T shirt. Then when I tried to ride back 'home' to the Civic Center Flea Bag Hotel in San Francisco, the back brake went out cuz the cotter and clevis pin fell outta the mechanical rear brake linkage at the toll booth on the Bay Bridge and luckily, I fixed it with a giant paperclip that was layin' on the ground.

So on the Bike Front things were still nice and fun in the Bay Area, riding all over the place with Steve a lot of the time, up Mount Tam north of the city and Mount Diablo on the east side, over to the redwoods in Muir Woods, we rode to the little secret hidden hippie town called Bolinas, and down into the South Bay some with a little ride down to Monterey and Carmel.

On the Home Front I'm still living in the flea bag roach hotel, and I had ventured out to a coupla other flea bag hotels but I liked Civic Center the best, ain't that sad, but at least I was still crab-free, so I had that going for me, which was good. And on the Work Front, things were still going OK in early November. My first work partner Mister Kuro Saki had taken off for Tokyo after we finished the Rotunda woodwork and my new partner was an older Mexican fellow named Bert. When the boss first hooked me up with him I asked Bert if his name was short for Roberto. He said "No Dave. My name is Norbert. Did ya ever know a Mexican named Norbert?"

I said nope, and we both kinda laughed and got along just fine the next few days. But those days were numbered and I had no idea.

The Wednesday the day before Thanksgiving Bert and me were working on the main floor at Neiman's. Where the escalators come down and land on the white marble floor is right in the middle of the action in the store. And right in the middle of that action is what Bert and me were working on, the big ass Godiva Chocolate Counter which wrapped all the way around the east escalator landing. These were very fancy showcases made of white woodwork with brass and beveled glass air-conditioned candy counters and were kinda involved and it was fun work. Then that fateful morning, while I was down on my knees on the marble floor cutting access holes in the bottoms of the cabinet bases to run electrical conduit through, the two big bosses Pete and Mac came up at the end of the counter and threw their plans and paperwork on the candy counters I had been working on. There was a column between them and me so I was kinda hidden. I kept quiet and unfortunately found out they were making out their Lay Off List. It was time to cut the crew down.

Now I thought I was in pretty good with Pete, the superintendent cuz I had worked for him before on three different Neiman's stores before in the late 1970s, their two stores in Dallas and the one in Fort Worth. Mac was a retired Air Force Colonel and maybe he didn't like my dope smokin' butt so hot even though we were both from Texas. But Pete had the last say over Mac, see? I thought I had Pete on my side. I heard them making the layoff list, and I knew the guys that were getting cut. Then Mac asked Pete, "What about Bert and Dave?" And then Pete sez "Well Mac, Bert is a good family man, and Dave is single. Dave can go find another job with no problem, so we'll keep Bert and let Dave go." Gulp.

Bert was a funny little guy who dressed in kinda rags and drove an old beat up mid 1970s Chevy station wagon. I was the new kid with the fancy chopper. What Pete and Mac did not know about Bert was the fact he had four (yes 4, not a typo) houses bought and paid for in San Francisco, his kids were already grown and he was probably worth more than both of them put together, bwah ha-ha. So Bert got to stay and Pete gave the other guys and me the Bad News that afternoon. So now I'm unemployed again, stuck in San Francisco with the chopper and toolbox there, with my other stuff up in the little storage unit in Wenatchee Washington. This is the last picture I took before I left San Francisco. It might look like it was taken from a plane, but it's up on top of Twin Peaks where I'd go to smoke Marys-ju-ana, looking out toward the Bay Bridge and Oakland over on the other side of the Bay.

Here's a few of my old 1980s San Francisco T shirts. We got here the awesome "Don't Be A Dickhead Come to Frisco Choppers" shirt, and the "Free Sonny Barger" shirt, the original Frisco Choppers Wings shirt with the only address on Valencia Street,...which sez "Still in the Ghetto", the Frisco Choppers Skull shirt, and we have a Dudley Perkins Alcatraz shirt and one from a joint called "Escape From New York Pizza" which was a cool pizza joint in the Upper Haight which was always open after bar time, owned by a guy named Marco who also rode a Shovelhead. And then there's the back sides.

Chapter 41:

END OF NOVEMBER-DECEMBER 1982

So, I got laid off the Wednesday before Thanksgiving. Bummer. But I wasn't the only one, maybe a dozen of us got the axe. And I'd already had 9 years in the carpenter trade by then and I was used to getting laid off. It was like my carpenter dad used to say when they'd lay him off,…"Well they ain't gettin' no cherry." Ya get used to it. You have to.

But the difference this time is, while the other guys can go get their trucks and cars out of the parking lots and load up their tools and head to their houses or apartments, I can't, cuz I ain't got no car or truck or house or apartment, and now I ain't even got a job. I'm suddenly in a fuckin' pickle like somebody just hit me in the face with a fresh cow pattie. So, I asked Pete if I could leave my toolbox on the job till the next Monday morning, since I rode the chopper in to work that day and couldn't haul the tools out. See what I did there? I didn't let ol' Pete know I was homeless livin' in a flea bag hotel. He probably thought I'd drive a nice pick up truck in the next Monday and take my tools to a real home. Anyhow, he fell for it and said sure, come pick 'em up Monday morning, so I was safe and that bought me a few days' time to figure out what the fuck to do next.

Wednesday after work I rode the chopper back up to my old flea bag hotel neighborhood by Market and Van Ness, to Dudley Perkins HD dealer which was at 66 Page Street back then. Right across the street from Dudley's was a big old building that had been converted into a storage facility, so I got a little storage cell for the tool-box. Now how do I get the toolbox there? Thanksgiving weekend came and went fot me kinda miserable. Early Monday morning I walked outta the stinky Civic Center Hotel dive and jumped on one of those old antique street cars and rode it down by Union Square. I went into Neiman's before the crew got to work. Some of the guys didn't know I had gotten the axe, and it was kinda embarrassing going through all the layoff news again, so I pushed my toolbox out onto the sidewalk. Now to trick a cabbie into doing what I needed done.

Back then in 1982 there were no SUVs for cabs, only cars and station wagons, so I had to wait until I saw a station wagon come by Union Square. I got one to stop, told him I'd give him 20 bucks to take me up Market to Dudley Perkins shop. He grinned really big like I was an out-of-town fool paying 20 bucks for a 5-minute drive, but then I showed him the toolbox he's gotta haul, ha-ha. After some talking and flashing the 20, he eventually went for it. I got the toolbox into the storage unit. Whew.

So now I've got all my boxes of chopper parts, the stereo, records, TV, clothes and other stuff up in a storage building in Wenatchee Washington, my toolbox is in a storage building in San Francisco, I've got no house or apartment to live in, plus my Texas driver's license and Texas license tag are gonna be expiring in a few more weeks, plus rent is gonna be due on the storage building in Wenatchee. And I ain't got no money in any bank cuz ya gotta have an address and phone number to get a bank account, right?

Now I got some wads of cash in my pockets, and that's about it, and it's disappearing…. I gotta do something quick. But what? I spent the next several days ridin' the chopper around Frisco looking for another jobbie-job, but no luck. Early 1980s sucked for construction work and besides, half the jobs I did back then were either department stores or hotels and those places do not want construction guys in their buildings during the holidays, they want cash paying customers and us gone.

December 25, I bought a nice sized bottle of Jose Cuervo and rode over to my Shovelhead riding partner Steve's apartment in Oakland and spent Christmas with him and his sister, her husband and their little daughter. January is coming, my Texas license crap is expiring, I gotta get outta San Francisco. I rode the chopper down to the Unemployment Office in Frisco and gave them Dane & Stacey's address up in Ellensburg to mail my future unemployment checks to, which were only 166 bucks a week. I called the 3 companies I had worked for to give them the same address to mail my W-2s, and Dane & Stacey don't have any idea I am coming to visit, bwah ha-ha. I don't know how many of you have ever complicated your Unemployment Check situation with those fuckin' Interstate Claims, but now I gotta do a 3 Way Claim. Sheeesh! More paperwork. I had worked in Dallas during January & February 1982, worked in Wenatchee March and April, got laid off and was unemployed until August, and then worked in California from August through November, and now I'm unemployed again, so things got very complicated.

I stashed my new Frisco Choppers, Dudley's and Arlen Ness T shirts and white carpenter overalls in the storage unit with the toolbox, then I packed the sleeping bag and tent on the chopper, did a big ass puff or three of nice Mendocino weed, kicked the chopper over, pointed the wide glide at the Golden Gate Bridge and took off back up to Washington,.......in January 1983. Kinda cold ride, yikes. This picture here is out on I-5, freezing my ass off in Northern California headed back up to Ellensburg. And nobody in Ellensburg even has a clue I am coming to,.....'visit',...shall we say? That's a nicer word than 'bum',.....right?

Chapter 42:

JANUARY 1983 HEADED BACK UP TO ELLENSBURG

This here is my First Ever Action Selfie, ha ha-ha. Yep, this was on the way up I-5 North ridin' from California up to Washington State. I carefully balanced the Canon camera on top of a fence post, set the timer for 10 seconds, then ran over to kick the Shovel over, and once it started then I had to run back over to the camera and grab it before it fell off the post from all the ground shaking cuz of the awesome stroker motor idling, ha-ha. (Not really, but it sounded good, eh?) And some people think us chopper hobos were never very busy? This was multi-tasking before they even invented the word.

We left off riding the 74 AMF Shovel Chop outta Frisco headed back up to Ellensburg on I-5 North to make an unexpected visit on my friends up there, yikes. It was cold. I knew it was gonna be cold, but I had to do it. But at least it wasn't raining, hah. Normally when I rode I-5 back then I could make the 850-mile ride in 2 days with no sweat. But since this was gonna be a cold ass ride and since I had some cash, I broke the ride into 3 days, averaging a little under 300 miles a day in the cold shit, and I wimped out and stayed in two nice warm road side motels along the way.

I made it through Redding and rode on up past snow-covered Mount Shasta to Yreka and got a room for the night and took a nice hot shower and slept on a bed much nicer than the one I had in the flea bag Civic Center Hotel, ha ha-ha. The next morning after breakfast and gassing up the chopper and checking the oil, I took off for the Oregon border. I rode acrost the border still on I-5 and then putted on through Ashland and Medford, then pushed on to Grants Pass for a rest stop.

Now here is where the story gets a little bit foggy for me, as for the details, ha-ha. Just off I-5, like down on the service road, was a bike shop and I stopped in at this independent bike shop in Grant's Pass, and for the life of me, cannot remember the name of the shop. But the guy who ran the place was called Big Chuck. How do I remember that? Cuz after I got the pictures developed in Ellensburg a few days later, I wrote Big Chuck's name on the back so I'd remember it nearly 40 years later, hahaha. Big Chuck's shop also had a very unusual bike in their front window......a Double Engine Rigid Shovelhead. How's that for different? Maybe some of you folks reading this might remember Big Chuck, his shop, or that bike from 1983?

For some reason beyond me right now, I wound up buying a new 21-inch Avon Speedmaster front tire. Don't ask me why, cuz I don't know why. I did not have a flat or blow out. Maybe it was a good deal and they talked me into it? And why would I buy just a front tire and not a back one? They wore out at the same time, right? And since I was living on the road and did not have a place to change the tire myself, why didn't I have Big Chuck do it right then and there? I don't know. All I remember is leaving their shop and I rode along with a new tire slung across my neck, over my right shoulder with my left arm sticking through it so I could still work the stick shift.

OK now I'm gonna give you 4 pictures from this stage of the trip. A picture of Mount Shasta with snow on it, and Big Chuck is sitting there on his stool working on a nice old Panhead, the Double Engine Shovelhead in their front window, and another boring selfie of me standing in some of that white snow shit, just to let ya know it really was cold on this here road trip, hardy har har.

We left off last time leaving the road side motel in Yreka California and freezing my butt off riding up I-5 into Grants Pass Oregon where I stopped in at a little bike shop, I can't remember the name of, but Big Chuck owned it. And for some reason I bought a new front 21-inch Avon tire from him, don't remember why, but I took it with me looped around my neck.

It was still cold ass ridin' cuz it was still cold ass January, hah. I rode on through Roseburg, then Eugene, then Corvallis and into Salem where I stopped for the night. Got 'nuther motel to keep from freezing, ain't no tent campin' for me on this road trip, ha ha-ha, cuz I wimped out. I only stopped for gas and eats and to puff on the green bud some. That's what kept me going, green bud power

In the motel room that night I rolled a coupla more joints for the next day's ride and got out my little Rand McNally Road Atlas booklet that had all the states and then I figured out the distance I had ridden and how much further I had to go. I had covered just under 700 miles in two days, not too bad considering the cold. The next morning after a nice hot filling breakfast and coffee for me and gas for the chopper, I did a puff or two and started out again. Oh,...and one funny thing about getting gas in Oregon back then,...it was illegal to fill your own tank. So every time I pulled in for gas, some 'stranger' had to fill the tank for me while I'd check the oil and chain tension.

I still had about 250 miles or so to make it to Ellensburg, where I was gonna drop in unexpectedly on my old ridin' buddies. What a fuckin' bum I was, eh? So I kicked the chopper over and pulled outta Salem that morning and pointed the wide glide to the north to go to Portland. When I got to Portland this time, instead of riding east on I-84 out to The Dalles which woulda been retracing my route I took back in July 1982, I kept riding I-5 North this time, crossing the Columbia River finally getting back into Washington State now.

After a little while, I peeled off on beautiful but cold ass HIghway 12 which meanders through the mountains of Mount Rainier National Park and gets fairly close to Mount Rainier, and that's where I took this picture of that big ass snow covered bumpy volcano. And now I'm getting pretty close to Ellensburg, ready to see some old friends. Correction: They weren't really 'old' friends cuz I'd only known them since May of 1980 and we were still in our 20s, but you get the drift. I'll say they were the oldest friends and riding buddies that I had on the west coast, how's that one?

Riding right by snowy Mount Rainier. I ain't gonna lie, my hands and nose were fuckin' freezin' on this trip and I had just about had enough of the cold ass shit, C'mon Ellensburg, show up soon! And eventually it did, a coupla hours later. Whew. But just because I got to Ellensburg don't mean it was any warmer, hahaha.

The address I had given for my W-2s and Unemployment Checks to be mailed to was Dane & Stacey's place. But since they had two little girls I didn't wanna barge in on them all unexpected like, ya know? So my first stop in Ellensburg was at Chuck's place, and Chuck is my old Rigid Shovel ridin' buddy on his Black 75. I had lost contact with Chuck until last year when I found him on FB, of all places. We started gabbing like crazy going back and forth on here, cuz we hadn't seen each other since 1988. And then Chuck mentioned the time I rode into Ellensburg in the dead of winter and showed up at his house with the front tire around my neck.

I had totally forgotten about that. I even asked him if he was sure it was me and not somebody else. Chuck said of course it was me. I still didn't really remember it. Then Chuck sent me this picture right here, a picture I had never seen before in my life, ha ha-ha. And,.....there's the spare tire, so I got busted not remembering it. Once I saw the picture Chuck had, I felt kinda goofy like. I was probably high as a kite, cuz why not, right? So I asked Chuck, "What did I do next? Come barging into yours and Jodi's place, eat up all your food, drink up your Tanqueray Gin, burp, then sit on the couch and fire up a joint?" I was joking, but Chuck said, "That's about what happened" Oh the embarrassment. And it even gets worse.

Then Chuck said I went back out to the bike, kicked it over while he took this picture, then I rode it up a plank into their living room. And next we put the bike up on a concrete cinder block and yanked the front wheel off and changed the tire right there in their living room. And that is the story of this picture I hadn't ever seen before. Now ain't ya glad I never came to visit you?

I crashed that first night at Chuck's & Jodi's place. The next day I had to haul rectum over to Wenatchee, over Blewett Pass......which means more cold riding up in the high mountains, not just down on the ground. The rent was due on the storage unit there and I gotta get over there quick to pay it. I packed the tent and sleeping bag on the chopper and took off for Wenatchee.

Ya know how when you're out on a road trip all alone, how your mind can sometimes wander? I was having sort of a meltdown on the way over Blewett, asking myself tricky unanswerable questions like "What the fuck am I doing? How did it all get this bad? Where am I going?" Just three years earlier, I had been a semi-respectful tax paying citizen in Dallas, owning my own house, riding a fancy chopper I built myself, cruising around in a custom-made Vette. And now? I lost it all in 18 months, the house money was gone, the Vette was gone, and I didn't even get to enjoy the fun of having a gambling addiction

I was sooo scattered, I was nearly falling apart. My carpenter toolbox was down in a storage unit in San Francisco, all my other stuff is over in Wenatchee and here I am, riding along on the only thing I have left, freezing my ass off, hoping the chopper hung together. I mean, just think how traumatizing a break down would be at this sordid stage? No cell phone's? No AAA Emergency Road Service, hahaha? But Joe Cox put together an excellent motor and tranny for me and my 24-year-old butt somehow managed to build a road worthy chopper that was taking whatever punishment I could dish out to it.

So I guess everything was OK in that department. Yet, I still had no place to live and not only no job, but not even a chance or whisper of a job, and I'm spread out in two different states, and to compound matters even more, I'm still flying the Texas license tag on the back of the chopper and still have a Texas driver's license which is getting ready to expire in just a few more days. That means when I left Texas in early spring of 1980, I had somehow managed to keep a valid Texas driver's license and tag sticker on it all the way up to January of 1983 and I didn't even live in Texas. Try some of that action today, eh?

This photo here is on the way to Wenatchee, up on top of Blewett Pass.

Riding over Blewett Pass from Ellensburg headed to Wenatchee it was a cold ride, but at least it wasn't raining or snowing,.....just yet. I shoulda left Ellensburg a little earlier in the day, cuz I was running outta sunlight which made it colder. There ain't that much sun light in Washington in the winter time. But the pay off is longer days in the summer,...right?

And if you were a crow and you wanted to fly from Ellensburg to Wenatchee, it wouldn't be that long of a trip over the big ridge. But if you are riding there, you got extra distance to cover. From Ellensburg you gotta do the beautiful ride north on Highway 97 and go up and over the pass, zig zagging back and forth through the hills like the river running beside you, and you actually go further north than Wenatchee sits. Then coming down off the pass you hit Highway 2, and ya gotta make a sharp turn to the right, like maybe 120 degrees, and then ride through Cashmere and Sunnyslope to get to Wenatchee. Now you know where we're headed.

By the time I came down off the pass and turned toward Wenatchee on Highway 2 it was getting pretty dark and the snow started falling,.....just great, eh? And the closer I got to Wenatchee the bigger the snowflakes got. I had no idea where I was gonna crash for the night, but my 'Number 1 Try' was gonna be my old buddy Reed the Carpet Layer's place. He was the guy I worked with and had my Unemployment Checks mailed to and was also the place where I was broke down for a week in his back yard when the plastic float bowl on the Lectron carb broke, ha ha-ha. And since I hadn't been back up Washington since July 1982, maybe he wouldn't mind me crashing there again?

Riding into Wenatchee I headed down the main drag, going to Reed's. But then, something saved Reed from my uninvited visit and that something was the long extended chrome Harley springer shining in the snowy street light that was the unmistakable front end of Ghost Rider Taz's Panhead Chopper, YAY! And there were a coupla other bikes there, too, collecting snow on their seats.

Just as I pulled up and started backing into the curb next to Taz's chop, I shut off my motor and out of the corner of my eye I saw the tavern door swing open and a little group of guys came out, laughing at me. Taz yelled out something like 'who in their right mind would be out riding a motorcycle on a night like this?' I pointed to their bikes and yelled back "You guys?" So we did a Howdy Guys Puff right there on the sidewalk, then went inside the nice warm bar and shot pool and drank beer until bar time. Then Taz invited me to crash on his couch that night, so I did. Reed got to keep sleeping and never even knew how close he came to getting rousted that night, hah.

The next day I rode over the Columbia River to East Wenatchee and paid the rent for the next 3 months on the storage unit where all my stuff was. And this musta been a Saturday cuz the folks' houses and apartments I stopped by to visit were home, so that was nice. I rode by Kenny & Darlene's place, then over to Sportster Jim & Debbie's, and Dan was there that we had worked with in the cabinet shop where I made a whoppin' 6 bucks an hour. I told them of this strange and far away magic place where I had been, called Sunny Californy, where I had been making 21 bucks an hour. Jim looked at me with a dead pan look and sez "So why the hell didya come back here? To freeze your ass off" I sez "I dunno, to see you guys I guess?" We all laughed and smoked some green bud. I crashed that night at their place.

The next day I said my thanks and goodbyes, left them some bud, packed the road gear on the chopper and rode back over Blewett Pass back to Ellensburg and this time I stopped at Dane & Stacey's place. Dane was a ranch hand and they lived on that ranch on the outside edge of town. As a matter of fact, they were the last house on the power grid system, they had no neighbors except for cows. And this here is Dane's Famous 1 Kick Pan, chopped in a swing arm frame.

After I left Wenatchee and rode back to Ellensburg, I forced myself upon Dane & Stacey, two of the nicest people in the world, and they had two little girls. I filled them in on how I used their address to have my Unemployment Checks mailed to, along with the three W-2 Forms that would be coming soon to do taxes. See there? I might be a homeless hobo, but I am still a tax paying citizen, bwahaha.

Dane called up Chuck and Mushroom Tim and they came over on their black choppers for some fun. Chuck's is the Black 75 Shovel and Tim's is the Black Panhead. We all rode black choppers back then,..... cuz what other color was there? Oh, and there's the ol' 74 AMF Chopper along with the others.

I'm back in Ellensburg thankfully staying at Dane & Stacey's place on the outside edge of town. They were sooo nice to me. I even had my own room, that's right. No sleeping on the floor, or out in the barn, or in a garage or tent. There was a bed in the room and the whole bit, like normal people lived, hahaha.

And now since I ain't a tent livin' Sasquatch anymore, actually living indoors, I did something else that might just blow away the folks who have been keeping up with this saga. February my Texas driver's license was expiring and so was my Texas license tag I had been running on the back since the build of 1979-80 winter in Dallas. Now it was time to either shit or get off the pot.

I actually went down to the Washington State Patrol office in Ellensburg and,.....gasp! Got a fuckin' Washington State Title and tag and then I got my driver's license. I had the title to the 74 AMF Chopper over in the storage unit in Wenatchee so I had brought that along with me. And mind you, the paperwork I have on the chopper is the original paperwork from the dealer July 11, 1974. So no cop can ever question who owns it. I used Dane & Stacey's address for that,.....oooops. I can say that all these years later,...right?

Now for all you folks who live in normal states that have a Department of Motor Vehicles, lemme inform ya right now that Washington State ain't got them. Nope. No sir-eee. You gotta go to the State Patrol and have them go over your chopper. They will go over it with a fine-tooth comb, a big ass flashlight and magnifying glass looking for anything they can deem "suspicious or stolen" so's they can impound your chopper. That is fact and most folks who build and ride choppers and lives there has their own title/tag horror stories. And since the Wenatchee State Patrol are such assholes, I was able to get it all done in Ellensburg without too much trouble.

And now, although I don't have my own apartment or house, on their books I am now a certified legal Washington State resident, after avoiding it for 3 years. Oh and get this funny shit. After your chopper passes and the State Troopers give you your paperwork to get the title and tag, then you gotta go to a sporting goods store to get your license tag. That is a fact. And then they will mail you a new title from Olympia. So my friends, feast your eyes on my brand fuckin' new Washington State License Tag, ...yay, and have a puff or three. Chuck and me had a few puffs up on this ridge overlooking Ellensburg and there's that brand new white and green Washington license tag on the back of the 74 AMF Chopper.

Chapter 43:

SKINNY BILL'S AND FAT MARY'S PLACE

Behold. This is what history looks like while it is still being created. This is Mister Jerry Webb. In order to protect the guilty as well as the innocent, I usually don't use the folks' last names in these stories, but since Jerry has "Webb" on his cut-off and since everybody in Central Washington already knows who he is, here we go with the details.

At this time I had just turned 28 years old and Jerry's a few years older than me, and that's cuz he is one of the Original Chopper Pilots from the 1960s. He is Chopper Royalty in my book. When I first tried to take this photo, Jerry laughed at me, waved his hand in the air like he was brushin' off a pesky fly or skeeter and said for me to get the hell outta here with that damn camera. I said "Jerry, I just GOTTA take this picture, you got no idea how fuckin' cool you are standing there next to your red Panhead."

So I took the picture and a few days later when I got these developed, I saw exactly what a cool ass photo it is. This is probably my favorite photo I ever took of anybody in motorsickle world. Just look how handsome and distinctive he is, hahaha, standing there wearing his cap and old road worn jacket with cut off, holding his beer right next to his beloved Red Pan/Shovel Chopper with that big "V" in the tank emblem shootin' up. Why this coulda been on the cover of Gentleman's Quarterly, hahaha,...if there is such a magazine,...or at least Easyriders, right? And then I found out Jerry's birthday was coming up in a few days, so I went back to the camera shop in Ellensburg and had them blow this photo up into an 8 X 10 glossy and then I put it in a nice frame and secretly gave it to Jerry's ol' lady so she could surprise him with it on his birthday.

This picture was shot at the wing ding thrown by Skinny Bill & Fat Mary at their place in Kittitas, just outside Ellensburg. I don't know if Jerry is still with us today or not, I sure hope so. He'd probably be in his 80s now. Jerry always had that glint in his eye and a wry suspicious grin like he was up to no good. That's what made me like him right off the bat. He's one of those rare guys I appreciated the first minute I listened to him and he also reminded me of Waylon Jennings. Now remember this Red Chopper cuz it is gonna play a very important part in the soon upcoming chapters, OK? It's a great pic if I don't mind saying so myself. Plus, as an added bonus, those are my fishtails sticking up in back.

I know it's still February and it ain't officially spring yet, but this is when it happened, cuz I'm gonna leave town come the first of March.

We got here the line up of a few of the bikes. Jerry's Red Pan/Shovel is on the end, next to that one is Chuck's 75 Rigid Shovel with the Dual Throat S&S, then there's my black wide glide front end sticking out with the chrome drum brake on it, then we have Skinny Bill's Flathead 45 with the two steel tractor seats on it, and then I think that is Ghost Rider Bob's Shovel on the end with the disc brake on front.

And then we got other viewpoints of the action with the grill going, good eats and cold frosty-ass beers which was easy to keep cold since it WAS cold, bwahaha. And yes, I still have the T shirt from this run.

If you've been following this drivel for very long, you probably remember me mentioning Ghost Rider Taz from Wenatchee. Ya see, him and me had something in common. We both lived in Wenatchee but liked to party with the Ellensburg crowd. For some reason still unknown to me, although it had about 1/4th the population of Wenatchee, Ellensburg seemed to have twice as many choppers as Wenatchee did. The Ghost Riders MC was a Central Washington Chapter so they covered both towns and the area in between.

Taz was my main riding guy in Wenatchee, plus pool shootin' partner, beer drinking buddy, fellow dope smoking fiend, and general all around town good hell-raiser who'd even let me crash at his place. And this is Taz and his Panhead Chopper.

And before anyone goes off about our front fenders, it was the law. Taz is the guy standing back in the right hand corner of the photo looking at the camera with his shades on and this is the only picture of his Pan and him that I ever got, dang it. And now that you've seen his long chrome springer front end, you can understand why it stuck out in the snowy night under the street lights when I rode into Wenatchee the week or so before.

We are at Skinny Bill's and Fat Mary's place in Kittitas Washington for their brand new First Annual Spring Opener Run that they still hold today. It was at their place that Dane was talking with Jerry about doing a frame swap on their Panheads. Jerry was ready to get rid of his rigid frame and go for a swing arm and Dane was ready to put his Pan motor in a rigid, so the deal was set up. Dane's swing arm already had the neck raked for his longer front end and it looked like both frames would work for both their extended Harley glide forks.

Chapter 44:

Dane and Stacy's Place

When I first met Dane & Stacey back in early spring of 1980, they were riding a chopped rigid frame 1964 Sportster. And now Dane wanted to get back to a rigid frame. Jerry got his Pan/Shovel pulled apart first and that Saturday afternoon brought his red rigid frame and its oil tank over to Dane's & Stacey's in his pick up truck and Dane stuck them out in his barn. After Jerry left, Dane and me kinda hemmed and hawed a little bit and then Dane decided there was no time like the present, so we started in on his Panhead.

We got a nice fire going in Dane's 55 gallon drum, this is the middle of February after all, and we got the Ellensburg Central Washington University Radio Station dialed in with some good rock & roll, we had good weed, we had lots of those generic white cans that said BEER on the sides, plus,...but wait there's more,... we had lots of Schmidt Animal Beer, the cans with the different animals on it. In other words, good weed and cheap beer and here we go, gonna start in building a chopper in one night. The fire got going good and so did we.

We got Dane's Panhead jacked up in the air high enough to drop the glide front end out, then Dane went to work unbolting everything else. Meanwhile I started in on Jerry's red rigid Harley frame, hitting it with lots of Gunk and wiping it down with towels, looking it over really good to see if there were any cracks. It checked out OK, so I started in lightly sanding it. Dane was gonna use Jerry's existing red paint as the primer cuz it was still in good shape, plus we would get done quicker.

On into the night we worked, pot smoke filling the air, rock & roll tunes filling our ears, beer filling our guts. While Dane kept up the dismantling of his beloved swing arm Pan, I started in with the rattle cans of gloss black. I gave it ultra light coats in order for it to dry fairly quick in the barn cuz the temperature was probably in the 20s outside. Around midnight, Stacey came out to the barn and she had a plate full of fresh warm brownies she just took outta the oven, and man did they hit the spot. We ate nearly the entire plate which meant there wasn't much for their two little girls the next day, hahaha. Oh well. Whaddaya gonna do?

We got back to the work when the Brownie Break was over. On into the night we went, 2 o'clock, more weed, 3 o'clock, more BEER, 4:30 AM, we kept going, building up the new black rigid frame chopper. Dane used his existing gas tank and both fenders cuz they already had nice matching paint on them. After the motor, tranny, and other parts were on, along with Jerry's rigid frame oil tank, we finally got the front end back on and then went to work wiring the puppy up. When the sun came up that Sunday morning, Dane kicked over his One Kick Panhead and it also became known in town as Dane's One Night Panhead.

Here's the pictures of Dane with his Panhead in the swing arm, the tear down shot, the rattle can black frame, and the newly finished chopper the next morning, complete with open belt drive, suicide clutch and a glass door knob for the shifter handle. Now how classy is that? And don't Dane look kinda like Jeff Lynne from Electric Light Orchestra?

After we built Dane's One Kick Pan Chopper in his barn in just one night, we had fun riding around town with the rest of the guys even though it was still kinda coldish. One memory that sticks out in my mind at this time is when our group of chopper people was down at the Ugly Bear Tavern shootin' pool and swillin' suds. All was going fine until Stacey suddenly came over by me in a mild state of panic and said "Dave, I think you're getting a ticket outside." I had parked the 74 AMF Chopper on the sidewalk in front of the bar and that was a big no-no in that town. Hell, I had been used to parking where ever I wanted in Frisco and never got any tickets. I even chained up the bike to the No Parking sign in front of the Civic Center Roach Hotel.

Well, I ventured on out to look at the bike and sure enough, Stacey was right. There was a ticket stuck to the chopper. I picked it up to read it and would ya believe, the grand total for parking on the sidewalk in Ellensburg Washington was 1 Whole Dollar? Yes, $1.00 total for a ticket, not a typo. Don't ya miss them prices today?

Meanwhile, back on the homeless front, the Unemployment Checks were coming in just fine to Dane & Stacey's place and what's more exciting is the income tax returns came in, so I was set, if you can still consider it being 'set' with no place to live, no car, and no jobbie-job. It was time to make a hard decision. The carpenter toolbox is still down in the storage building acrost the street from Dudley Perkins HD shop, all my other stuff is still over in the Wenatchee storage building, and there I was, still in Ellensburg. I loved the folks in Ellensburg, but I knew I wasn't gonna get any type of job there that paid anything. Same for Wenatchee. I could maybe get a job down in Frisco, there were certainly more chances for work, but I knew very few people there. Hmm.....

I had to go think about it. So that meant riding back up to the ridge over-looking Ellensburg and having a smoke and think session with myself. And forget about riding out I-82 with all the truckers and heavier traffic, I rode out the old road, Highway 821 which snakes along nice and purdy right next to the river. This picture here is up on that ridge. Somehow,...someway,...I gotta get my shit together right now while I still have the income tax returns. If I blow this money, then I will be totally fucked. And hell no,...selling the Shovelhead is not an option, ha ha-ha.

I made the hard decision to go back to San Francisco even though I wanted to stay in Ellensburg. But first, I had one fun thing to do over in Wenatchee. I had seen some of the Ellensburg college kids with those things called The Walkman that played music, hahaha. Now before you roll your eyes and laugh and say I've gone yuppie and done gone Hollywood, lemme explain that I'm a die hard rock & roller and music is important to me and I hadn't got to play any of my records since September of 1981 cuz that's how long they'd been in the storage unit in Wenatchee, see? And I'm not riding a new bagger with 16 stereo speakers blastin' on it to annoy the squirrels and little old ladies, it's just a headpiece with ear phones.

I rode back over Blewett Pass again and went into Wenatchee, paid yet another month on the storage rent, which was now good to the end of April. Then I rode over to the music store and got a Walkman with my income tax return money,...yay! So now I had tunes again for the first time in about 18 months. And ya know what was really fun? Getting high and riding the chopper through the majestic Cascade Mountains while listening to Pink Floyd, that's what. Just think about that for a second. Snowcapped mountains, rivers pouring right outta rock cliffs on your right side, crashing river down on the left side, maybe an eagle or two soaring up i the sky, the rumble of a Shovelhead motor underneath you thrilling you to your bone marrow and now add Pink Floyd to the mix. It was awesome, I tell ya.

I made it back over the pass to Ellensburg that same day and some of the folks there laughed at me for getting a Walkman, but so what, I kept the Walkman down inside my jacket in the chest pocket, ran the cord up through the zipper in the neck and had the ear phones underneath either my Flaying Ace leather hat or the Harley sock hat, depending on how cold it was, and the little control doo-dad hung right in front where I could get to it easy. The other tapes in the tape holder case where ones like lots of folks used to make back then that we recorded on there ourselves. I made those tapes back in 1970s Dallas with all my favorite tunes, so I got to hear everything I liked and it was commercial free, so how's that? And for the younger crowd reading this, cassette tapes were the things made to play music before the CD things were made to play music before the iPod things were made to play music before your smart phone that plays music was invented.

And now it's time for me to start gearing up to leave all my good pals in Ellensburg, not knowing how long I would be gone. This picture here is the box of music, ready for The Walkman, batteries not included. And now I've got tunes.

This is the last picture I took of Chuck's and my Shovel Chops up on the high ridge where'd we ride sometimes. That is the snowy Mount Stuart peak in the background. At this stage I'm ready to make the big move back to California, if riding a chopper back down there can be considered a big move.

The storage unit that contains the busted Durfee girder, other chopper parts, tools and house items is paid through to the end of April. You know how those storage guys will sell all the stuff in your unit if you get behind, hahaha, and I didn't want all my worldly possessions going up for bid. My carpenter toolbox is still down in the storage unit across the street from Dudley Perkins HD dealer. And I'm still in Ellensburg.

It's about time to get my shit together and get all this menagerie of crap back together in one location like a normal human would try to do. I'm 28 years old at this stage and I was better off when I was 21. It's been a long downhill slide.

This day was the last Friday in February, the 25th, and tomorrow will be Saturday and the day I split back to San Francisco. Little did I know what terrors lay in wait for me out on the road the next day.

Woke up at Dane & Stacey's this Saturday morning and went through the road gear getting ready to roll out. A Chopper Hobo has to carry everything with him clothes-wise and be prepared for anything that might happen. It's a lot more fun being a hobo in the summer time, that's for sure. Jeans, T shirt, and a bandana are about all you need and it's fun riding. Being a hobo in the winter time is more serious business, ha ha-ha. And it's still February in the Pacific Northwest and sometimes that means getting dressed for the road can be be a chore in itself.

Usually on extra cold days on the bottom half I wore the basic BVDs, then long johns over that, then flannel lined jeans, then my Official Ellensburg Chaps over the top. And these chaps were the real deal, made from thick Ellensburg vat-dyed cow hides, stitched up at a local saddle shop. In other words, these were real heavy duty working cowboy items, not the skimpy little light weight designer chaps they sell in those High Dollar Motorcycle Boutiques today.

On my feet were the infamous heavy duty Nasty Feet Boots that I had ordered outta the back of an Easyriders mag back in the late 1970s in Dallas. And those boots, if anyone remembers, have the high tops that come up nearly to your knees, and the boot laces must be about 7 or 8 feet long. In other words, they were good serious heavy duty boots, steel toes, steel shanks for the road, or kicking in a car door if they got too close, hah. On top I wore a T shirt, then long johns, then a long sleeved flannel shirt, then my 1975 Harley AMF leather jacket, and this time of year I'd put the detachable furry collar on it. Goggles and heavy duty gloves with gauntlets finished it off. Now I was good to go.

After eating the big ol' tasty breakfast Stacey made, I moseyed out to the new pig pen Dane and I had built a few days before and I said farewell to all my little pig-puppies in the pen. They were maybe a month old, and if you ever played with little piggies, they are sorta like puppies except they are hard and solid like bricks. Then I played with their German Shepherd one last time. He was one cool funny dog. I used to rassle with him and he'd chew on my hands and arms and legs and I'd bite him on his ears and nose. It was a thing we did, hahaha.

It wasn't extra cold this day, maybe just medium cold, so I wrapped the chaps around the sleeping bag on front and decided I was gonna wear my Harley sock hat with the new Walkman ear phones instead of the Flying Ace leather hat, which was in the bag. But when I looked for the sock hat that I had set on the chopper's seat,..... it was gone. Now where the fuck did that thing go? I need it right now. I'm looking in front of, behind and under the chopper. Suddenly Stacey sez "What's the dog got over there by the tree? And we looked up and there was the dog shaking its head back and forth with something black in his mouth, and you guessed it,.....my black Harley sock hat. I had to go rassle the dog again to get it back, bwahaha-ha. I think he did that on purpose. Geeze, I ain't ever gonna get outta here, eh?

So I shook the dog slobbers outta the now chewed up hole-ie hat, pulled it over my noggin with the new-fangled Walkman headphones, and pulled my big heavy duty gloves on. This was really sad saying good bye to such good people, but I gotta go. So I kicked over the 74 AMF, the pipes fired up, and I settled my Texas butt down in the familiar saddle where I'd be livin' the next few days. Pushed in the suicide clutch, slapped the stick shift back into 1st gear, let the clutch out kinda too fast on purpose and kicked up some dirt in their driveway on the way out. I waved bye to Dane and Stacey and their little girls one last time and headed on up the road wracking the fishtails off. I was headed toward Portland which would probably be about a 4- or 5-hour ride. The route I was taking would be I-82 through Yakima, on down to Toppenish, then split off on Highway 97 and head on down south toward the Columbia River then catch I-84 headed toward The Dalles, Oregon.

These pictures here are the last ones I took in Washington, sniff, sniff. We have three mountainside pictures and one of the dog slobbered chewed up sock hat.

Chapter 45:

THE BUSTED FRAME

So I ended up leaving Dane and Stacey's place that fateful Saturday morning, with hardly a care in the world,..... except for trying to stay warm while ridin' on a rigid frame chopper in February in the Pacific Northwest. After leaving Ellensburg, I made it through Yakima and Toppenish and on down to the Columbia River, crossed it and was now in Oregon. I stopped in at a gas station and while the guy filled the gas tank, I snuck around to the side of the station where the bathrooms were, took a leak and took a puff. There, now everything is just fine,...right? I rode on through The Dalles on i-84 when the damndest thing happened. It was sheer terror, I shit ya not.

Ya know how sometimes your mind can wander when you're out there on the highway all alone and ain't got nobody ridin' with you? Well that's what my brain was doing, just kinda in limbo, stoned, listening to the music on the Walkman, having fun in the cold. I'd look up the highway, then I'd look over to a mountain top, then look off to the other side at the river. Well for some reason I happened to be looking at the neck of my tastefully molded frame, with the nice black imron paint and the fancy red pinstripes when,.....it happened.

The fuckin' left side downtube broke right in half while I was staring at it. WHAT THE FUCK? Am I on 'shrooms? How the hell did that just happen? Am I seeing shit?

I went into Panic Mode. Pulled over onto the shoulder of the highway, shut the motor off, got off the bike. This kinda shit ain't even supposed to happen,.....right? But there it was, staring me right in the face. I reached out and felt it, as if my eyes were lyin' to me. Yep. Busted right in half. I tried to wiggle it. I wiggled. I did some quick Amateur Detective Work and thought I saw what caused it. When I built this version back in the winter of 1979-80, I had been reading all the chopper magazines, Easyriders, Street Choppers, Choppers, if you know what I mean? And in those mags they had some beautiful show bikes, and the guys that built those show bikes did what the mags called "Super Sano Wiring Jobs" on them, where they drilled little holes in the frame tubes and ran the wiring inside to hide it. Well,.....that's what my 24 year old butt had done back in the 1979-80 build.

So here I was, my now-28 year old butt stuck on the side of the highway in February of 1983, homeless, broke down on the side of the road with a busted frame downtube cuz I drilled a hole in the tube to run the fuckin' wiring in. Drilling holes might work for show bikes that don't get ridden very much, but now we have evidence of what happens in real life out on the road. SHITFUCKHELLPISS!

So what the fuck am I gonna do now? No choice but to keep riding. It's not like I can weld it right here and now, eh? So I kicked the chopper back to life, got back down in the seat and took off, this time instead of cruisin' along 60 or 65, I was puttin' along doing maybe 40 or so, cuz who wants to go any faster on a busted frame? All I could do was keep my eyes peeled for the next big logging truck stop to come along, and it needed to be on my side of the road. Is that too much to ask? Here's a picture of the busted frame. And don't worry, it gets even worse.

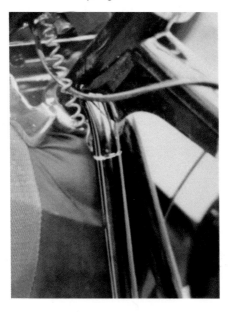

We left off last time with a busted frame downtube on the side of the road out east of Portland Oregon. After sitting on the bike and jumping up and down in the seat to see if anything else would happen, I deemed it 'Semi Road-Worthy', kicked it over and off I took, cuz,...umm,...what else could I do? I did not have a welder set up and generator with me, right?

I kept riding down the right side shoulder of I-84, limpin' along doin' maybe 40 mph or so while the semi-trucks and cars kept whizzin' by my busted ass.. As I rode along on the crippled chopper, my mind went wandering, wondering what the fuck has happened to me. I left Dallas as a 25-year-old young whippersnapper, almost three years ago. And when I left, I was on my brand-new 6th chopper build with new Imron paint, new motor and tranny build, new chrome, new tires and chain, new everything, with over 10 grand to my name, the legal money I got from selling the house, not doing an illegal drug deal with Phil Spector on the side of the road like Captain America and Billy did, bwahaha. In other words, I had been good, legal and honest,....right? Hahaha. And now this fuckin' shit?

I was turned down trying to buy two houses in Ellensburg cuz I didn't have an established work record, got laid of that job, moved to Wenatchee, got laid off there, got hit by a judge's granddaughter in her bird shit splattered junk yard VW Bug with no license tag and railroaded into court on a fake charge, had to sell the car cuz I needed the money to live on, tried to re-group first in Dallas, got laid off, and then again in San Francisco, where I got crabs and then got laid off that job the day before Thanksgiving, rode back up to Washington trying to re-goup again, didn't work out, and now I'm ridin' along on a limpin' chopper out in the middle of nowhere in northern Oregon with a busted frame tube. I could feel all my rancid guts bubblin' up inside me, ready to come violently spewing out my mouth.

I drew in a really deep breath. and for as long and loud as I could yell, I screamed out "FUUUUUUUUUUUUUUUUUCK!",..... to nobody there. But at least it made me feel better, plus I still had tunes and it wasn't raining, so I had that going for me, which was nice. And then?

Maybe 20 minutes or so from where the break happened, I saw a for-real truck stop coming up on the next exit ramp. Yay. What joy,...yawn. And truck stops back then in the Pacific Northwest were real truck stops, not these shitty so-called truck stops we have today that sell candy bars and micro waved frozen pizza, run by goons that have no idea how to fix anything. Hell, they wouldn't even know how to count out your change if the cash register didn't tell them how much it was,...right? Right.

Anyhow, I rode on down the exit ramp and pulled into the crunchy gravel parking lot where a coupla logging trucks were getting fuel. There were two guys working the place. I pulled up next to the older guy, shut the engine off, and asked him if he had a heliarc set up. He said "Of course." I asked "Do ya think you can fix this busted tube right here? "...pointing to it. He looked at it and said "Sure, pull your bike around to the back and you'll see the welding shop there, and pull your gas tank off." Then he went back to his customer. So, I pushed the loaded chopper around to the back side where his welding shop was.

I took off all the road gear and opened up my tool bag in back. I got out a screwdriver and removed the fuel line, then unbolted the two bolts that held on the gas tank. Next, I lifted the gas tank up, and then? And then I nearly shit my pants and threw up in my mouth at the same time. The backbone was also busted in half, right at the back of the front gusset.

So I had been feelin' all nice and high, having a great ride and good buzz going, listening to tunes on the Walkman, riding along doing around 60 or 65, and the only thing holding the entire bike together was the 1979 Paughco Mustang 3.2 gallon gas tank. The guy came walking back to the welding shop area and I said "I think I just doubled your work." I took this picture of the busted backbone.

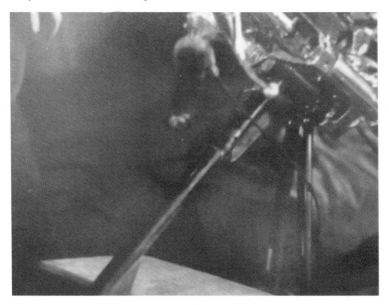

When the guy came back over to look at the broken back bone, I asked him "So whaddaya think we oughta do now?" He laughed. He said that's the shits, then pointed me to his humongous pile of scrap metal and old used pipes and other funky dirty shit in the back of his shop. See there? I told ya before this was a real truck stop, not some fancy boutique fake ass truck stop like they've got today.

He told me I needed to find a chunk of pipe that had the same inside diameter as the outside diameter of the frame back bone, then cut a chunk about 3 inches long or so, and then split it down the middle on both sides, to make a splint. My carpenter wood based brain immediately shifted into Metal Mode. So I went scroungin'. I was missing Dane and Stacey's trusty German Shepherd right now cuz he'd help me sniff one out, hah.

I finally found a chunk. Now remember this was 1983 so there ain't no battery powered Sawzalls or chop saws around, if you get my drift? That means,............ hacksaw,............ my favorite dependable non powered chopper tool to this day. So there I am, in the back of the shop with the chunk of pipe just hack sawin' away,..... puff, puff, puff. The walls of the pipe were probably 1/4 inch thick so I've got some serious sawin' to do. Then after I got it cut off, I put it in his big bench vise and split it down the middle, like a sausage on the grill, then I had to do the other side. I was now sweatin' my ass off, in February in Oregon. So maybe after 30 minutes or so of hack saw time, I finally had a specimen he liked. He clamped it on each side of the back bone and got his welder ready. As he put his face shield on, I quickly grabbed for a blanket he had a-layin' there so as to protect the nice chrome,...right?

Then when he started in welding, the sparks came down and set the blanket on fire, oh shit....I tried putting it out with my hands but that didn't work so good. I discovered right then and there that fire is hot. So next I tapped him on the shoulder so he'd stop for a bit and I yanked the blanket out. I replaced it with that chunk of plywood you see in this picture. Then he continued welding the back bone splint and next he welded the down tube and finally got done. Crackle,...sizzle,....popping noises,... the sounds of red hot molten metal cooling off. Sigh. Now my once pristine molded black imron paint and fancy red pin stripes are burnt to shit and now I got a rat bike. Oh joy.

He went back out to wait on customers while I put the chopper back together and loaded the road gear back on. As I pushed the bike out to his pump, I asked him what I owed him for his fine emergency repair. He said 20 bucks would do. I gave him 40, cuz why not? He got me going when it seemed hopeless and desperate. I filled up the gas tank at his pump, paid him for that, then kicked the chopper over and took off back down I-84 headed west. That breakdown and repair time musta been around 2 hours total, not bad, really. So now I had to make up for lost time. When I got over close to Portland, I caught I-5 and headed south, no more need for a map now until I get to the Bay Area.

I rode through Salem, then Corvallis came and went behind me. When I got to the Eugene area,.....guess what? Fuckin' rain. Oh great, exactly what I needed to make the day seem just right, why not? It was like the little cherry on top of a banana split. I got totally soaked and kept riding trying to make up for the breakdown time. I finally got as far as Roseburg and called it quits. Grabbed a motel room on the side of the road. That hot shower alone that night was worth the price of the room. Ain't it kinda sad when you hafta remember a simple thing like taking a shower was the best thing that happened to you that day? That night I snuck out and pulled the chopper in from the rain and let it sleep with me, poor thing. I did not get a picture of that, dammit, hah. I laid in the bed looking at its head light, talking to it. I still had a little bottle of Bacardi Run with me, so I moseyed out the door down to their ice machine and grabbed some ice and two Cokes. When I got back to the room, I rolled up a nice fat one and lit it up and put the Walkman head phones on. Maybe tomorrow will be a better day?

Chapter 46:

Racing the Excalibur

I t's a new day, yay! Sunday morning. And it can't possibly be any worse than the day before, right? Right. It had stopped raining now, which was good. I opened the door and pushed the chopper back out into the parking lot in front of my motel room as quiet as I could. Then I packed the road gear on it so it would look like it had been sitting there all night. This place had a little cafe so I had breakfast there.

From looking at the map at the distance left to San Francisco, it figured out to be around a full day's ride, around 450 miles. And it was still kinda cold. I had spread out the road gear and my extra clothes in the room the night before so everything was mostly dry, so that was good. Cold + wet together = no fun.

After eating I gassed up the chopper, checked the oil and chain and set off for the California border, which was about 2 & 1/2 hours away I guessed. I stayed on I-5 South through Grants Pass where Big Chuck's shop was that I had visited the trip before on the way up back in January. Then came Medford and Ashland and after that,...the border.

It was still before noon when I crossed into California, so that was good. About 3 or 4 hours into the trip that day, I was approaching Mount Shasta, which was still snow covered. I rode on up the pass and got over the top, then started back down the southern side when it happened.

No,..nuthin' broke. What happened was I saw a big white object floating up on the right side, beside me on the highway, and no, it was not a flying saucer. It was one of those Excalibur cars, long, low, white and mean looking, with the stainless steel exhausts curling out of the hood, running back down the side of the car. I looked over at the guy and he was grinning at me like he was the devil. He gunned his motor a bit, lurching back and forth. This devil guy wanted to race, bwah a ha-ha. OK, pal, it's on!

With my 1977 Easyriders magazine Nasty Feet boot heels, I kicked down the rear passenger pegs, the old metal #1 pegs I still run today. I hooked my heels over them, drew my knees in tight to the motor, laid down on the gas tank, sucked my elbows in and twisted that fuckin' throttle as far as it would go and I fuckin' held it there, letting all 86 inches scream out the fishtails and letting the Andrews tranny and 25 tooth counter shaft sprocket do what they were intended to do.

I pulled away from the Excalibur, he never even came up close. I still held the throttle wide fuckin' open. I had never heard those fishtails sound like that before and have never heard them sound like that since. It was orgasmic! That Joe Cox-built Shovel motor was screamin' itself as loud as it possibly could. With that throttle twisted all the way, I let out all the anxiety of the day before. All those gremlins and negative hobo thoughts blew right out the tail pipes. I was in heaven, and the devil was behind me.

But after maybe 1 to 2 minutes of that, I started wondering about that welding job from the day before, I didn't know that guy. Was he a good welder? Or was he a guy who simply fixed logging trucks the best he could? And then I started worrying about the chain.

What if the chain broke? What if it snapped and jammed up into the sprocket and locked me up on the road doing well over 100? What if? What if? What if? The 'what ifs' were driving me nuts now, so I rolled back off the throttle so's I wouldn't end up looking like a piece of crispy bacon, or even worse and smaller.

The Excalibur honked his horn as he sped on by me. This here is the picture I took at Mount Shasta right after the race. And yes, I was doing over a hunnerd with all this road gear packed on the front end. Not one fuckin' problem with packing on the front end, folks.

After racing the long white Excalibur down the south side of the 4,310 feet high Mount Shasta pass. I didn't get a checkered flag or even a beer for winning. Oh well. From there I still had about a 5 hours ride to go. That means I'd be ridin' into the Bay Area around sundown, which woulda been heavy traffic on a regular work day, but this was still Sunday.

When I got closer to the destination, I did my usual route pullin' off to the west from I-5 and headed over to Highway 101 to go into the city the Golden Gate Bridge way. Nothing unusual happened on the way into Frisco,...just the bridge supports over my head and the Pacific Ocean to the right of me, which was nice.

When I rolled into downtown, I automatically started riding over to the flea bag Civic Center Hotel, just outta habit, I suppose? And I actually pulled up in front of it, and then I thought to myself,...what the fuck am I doing? I don't wanna go backwards and live inside this flea bitten dump again. Then while I was sittin' there on the idlin' chopper, I thought about my good ol' Texas-born buddy, Oakland Steve and his Maroon Shovel. I remembered exactly where he lived, so off I went, forcing my Chopper Hobo self on yet another unsuspecting soul. How fuckin' rude, eh, wink, wink?

I got onto the familiar entrance to the Oakland Bay Bridge and let the motor wind out, leanin' through the big curve, headed on up the bridge. Traffic was light, so that was nice. Over the top and then down the other side and next it was blasting through the Treasure Island Tunnel, letting the fishtails wrack off good so the folks in the cars could hear 'em good. Shot out the other side of the tunnel, then the bridge curves a bit going into Oakland over their piers and docks. I took the exit and then another street that ran down toward Lake Merrit in Oakland, got close to where the lake is, then turned left away from the lake and rode past the Paramount Theater, then turned right, rode a short distance and turned left, and there I was. See there? 39 years later and I still remember how to get to Steve's place and now you do, too.

Steve's apartment building was on the left side of the street, a nice old two Storey brick building with 8 units, probably from the late 1920s or 30s, and while it did not have a garage in back, it did have a covered car port with 8 individual parking spots. I rode in the side driveway and sure enough, there was Steve's Maroon Shovel in his spot, and that meant he was probably there, cuz like me, he did not own a car. I rode up next to his bike and shut off the 74. About the time the chopper shut off,

Steve musta heard the racket and came out his back door with a big grin on his mug. He said "I don't believe it." I said "Hey there, Steve, how's it going?"

As he came walking up to me, I stuck out my hand but he brushed it aside and instead gave me a big ol' Texas Bear Hug like Fritz Von Erich woulda done, pattin' me on the back. And then suddenly he let go and with both hands pushed me in the chest away from him and yelled out "Where the fuck have you been?" I sez "Whaddaya mean?" He sez "I mean you've been gone since New Years, what the fuck happened to you?"

I told him I had to ride back up to Washington to pay rent on the storage, signed up for unemployment and had to go to Dane and Stacey's for the Unemployment Checks and my tax returns to be mailed to. In other words, I had to do it cuz I needed the money, hah. He was still semi-pissed off and sez "So you just rode away without saying anything to anybody. I had no idea what happened to you. I didn't know if you rode off a cliff into the ocean, got hit and killed by a car, or what happened. I even rode by that hotel to see where you were and and the guy there told me he hadn't seen you for a while."

Hmm,.....I guess I fucked up. I sez "Sorry about all that, but I'm here now." So next he seemed to settle down a bit and then asked me if I had eaten yet, I said nope, so he said there was a great Mexican joint a few blocks away. I said I was starving, let's go eat and told him I'd get him all the Mexican food and margaritas he could hold. He said "Lemme go get my keys." I asked "Can I leave my stuff here at your place?" Without thinking about it too much, he said yes, so I took the road gear off my bike and threw it inside his place.

See what I did there? Once a Chopper Hobo throws its road gear inside your place, that means it now lives there with you, like a skinny hungry tick just latched onto a nice juicy hound dog, hah. We kicked the two Shovels over. It was nice hearing them run together again. So we rode over to the Mexican joint and ate and drank a bunch of margaritas and then did some shots with limes and salt. Steve sure liked his Tequila. Burp. I ended up staying with Steve for a few days and when he rode off to work in the mornings, I'd ride over to Frisco and look for a place to live in The Haight. I also got to see my carpenter toolbox again when I went to pay rent on the storage unit across the street from Dudley's.

I don't have a photo of Steve and his Shovel at this point in time, not until we went camping in the Redwoods in the spring, so I'm gonna give ya this picture, "In Memory" of the once beautiful custom neck on the 74 AMF Chopper. Lots of work went into this custom hand-built frame. My 23-year-old self drew the neck, Dutch and George built it in their shop in Arlington Texas, I molded it inside my house, my Shovel buddy Terry sprayed it with black Imron paint in my garage, and it was pinstriped by Doctor Burns Emergency Pinstriping at a ride-in bike show and swap meet at the Arlington HD dealer, so 5 different people worked on it. Then I drilled little holes in the neck of the frame to run the wires through and that must be what weakened it and made it break these 3 years later.

RIP old frame neck.

Chapter 47:

No Longer a Chopper Hobo

Steve lettin' me crash at his place in Oakland was one of the nicest things any California person ever did for me. His place was very close to getting on the Oakland Bay Bridge, so in the mornings I'd leave his place and ride the chopper over to San Francisco and hit The Haight looking for a place to live.

I wanted to live in what they call the Upper Haight, on the west end of Haight Street down by Cole and Belvidere, where Haight ends at Golden Gate Park. The summer of 1982 I had lived down in the Lower Haight, in between Fillmore and Steiner, that's where I picked up all those nice crabs, for free, ha ha-ha.

So up on Haight Street west of Ashbury there was a nice old laundromat I had gone to before, called Haight Laundry. Get it? Pronounced 'Hate Laundry.' It was kinda close to one of the head shops I went to. Aside from being able to wash your clothes there, they also had one of those community cork boards on the wall, where people post cars for sale, lost dogs and cats, ads looking for work, and you guessed it, places for rent. It was here that I found the ad for a 2 bedroom flat with a garage just a few blocks away, for 'only' 500 bucks,...yikes. So I went to the pay phone,... remember those?,...and I called the number.

I met the landlord guy at the 2 story flat on Stanyan and Carl. Stanyan is the street that Haight Street dies into, right on the east edge of Golden Gate Park. If you've seen the old footage of the 1967 hippies dancing in Golden Gate Park and the Grateful Dead playing outside, this is right at that place.

The older guy, maybe mid 60s, showed up in his black Mercedes and parked in the driveway at the flat. He took a look at me in my leather jacket and the now-rat bike chopper sitting on the sidewalk and I think he may have had second thoughts, hahaha. But we started bullshittin' and I could tell it might work out OK and I might sucker this guy into,.....I mean,.....I might make a nice tenant for this genial fellow, hahaha.

It started out as an awkward conversation and my Texas drawl probably didn't work to my advantage. He asked me for rental or job references. Nope, I ain't got any. He asked me if I currently had a job. Nope, but I did work on the Neiman's store down at Union Square the summer and fall of 1982. Hmm. Did I have a bank account or a credit card or good credit rating? Nope, of course not, bwahaha. Well,... then where did I live while I was working the four months at Neimen's? Umm,...in the Civic Center Hotel. Yikes, that didn't score any points, either, he kinda wrinkled up his nose. I didn't have the heart to tell him my old address was The Green & Yellow Tent, Icicle River, Washington 98826. He mighta thought I was joking.

So I told him I had my carpenter toolbox stored in the building down on Page Street across from Dudleys and I was ready to go to work. I told him while I did not have any bank account yet, what I did have was,...umm,.....CASH! Suddenly it seemed like he liked me a little bit better. We went inside and checked out the place. It was one of those old 1910s Victorian homes with the 10 foot ceilings. The lots for houses in San Francisco are usually 25 feet wide and 100 feet deep. The garage is on the ground level, of course. And you usually walk up a few steps to get to the front security gate door that you open, then walk up a few more steps to go into the entrance. Then there are two more doors, one for the first floor and the other for the second floor, which is actually 3 floors up, ha ha-ha. Are you still with me? It's a lotta steps to get in those old houses. This is the typical way the Victorian houses there are set up, and they are jammed right next to each other, not even one inch in between.

The empty flat on the top floor kinda echoed when we walked through on the old timey hardwood floors. It had 1 bedroom in front, a living room with an old timey gas fireplace that he said did not work, a hallway going down to a bathroom with just the tub and sink, and then the toilet was in its own room, and then the other bedroom and a little dining room and kitchen in the back of the flat, with a washer and dryer on the back porch which actually had kind of a nice view looking out. There was a couple of twins down on the first floor, a guy and his twin sister and they were college students and didn't have a car,...so guess what? That means I got the whole garage to myself, ha ha-ha. The landlord dude let me have the flat.

I rode back over to Oakland and told Steve "Hey man, I ain't a homeless hobo anymore, I just signed a lease on a flat." I loaded up the road gear that was in Steve's place and packed it on the chopper to go to my new digs. Of course, I did not have even one stick of furniture with me it was still up in Wenatchee Washington. So my first night there, I threw the tent over in the corner of the front bedroom and rolled out my sleeping bag on the floor, right in front of the window which looked out at Stanyan Street and the Twin Peaks Hill, where the fog comes swirling in through the trees from off the ocean. It was a really cool flat in a really cool neighborhood with really cool hippie cafes and head shops. Since September 1981, I finally had my very own home,...yay! I used my leather jacket for a pillow just as I had for the past 18 months, hah. Then a funny thing happened.

Didya ever get the feelin' you were being stared at? I woke up the next morning feeling kinda uneasy. I was still a-layin' there on my back with my eyes closed, but I was awake. I got that feeling I was being stared at. I slowly opened my peepers and looked over to the right side where the window was. And there he was, a real life hobo sitting up on the fire escape staring right at me through the window, bwahahaha! Welcome to San Francisco, eh? I smiled and waved at him. He was an outside hobo, I was now an inside former hobo, only an 1/8th inch of thin windowpane of glass separated us two hobos. This is a picture of where I was sleeping on the floor the first night and out that window is where the hobo was perched.

Chapter 48:

Getting it Together Again

Keys! Gawddamn keys! My new landlord in the Haight Ashbury gave me 3 keys, one for the security gate, one for the front door to the upstairs unit which also worked on the back door, and one for the lock on the garage door . Now I ask ya, do you got any idea how long it had been since I had fuckin' keys to anything, hahaha? A looooong time. And before you start thinking the 74 AMF Chopper has a key, oh no it don't, never has and never will. I flip toggle switches, kick and go. If it ain't got a key, then you can't lose the key,...right?

So now I gotta protect and guard these 3 keys and hope like hell I don't lose 'em. I guess maybe that's the first worry a reformed hobo must face, at least in my case it was. OK so now I'm in the upstairs flat, the Shovel Chop is safe and sound down in the garage underneath me, chained up to a post in the garage. The carpenter toolbox is down in the storage unit acrost from Dudley's, and the busted Durfee girder and chopper parts and all my 1975 Technics stereo, albums, and other worldly possessions are still up in the little storage unit in Wenatchee. Things are looking up,.....maybe. Oh, and I rode down to Haight Street and went in the Wells Fargo Bank and opened a gawddamn checking account just like a normal person would, cuz it was looking like I'd need one again.

I got back 'home' (weird typing out that word at this stage) and then walked up to the street corner where there was a phone booth (remember them things?) that smelled like piss, and I called up Oakland Steve and gave him my new address. After he got off work he was gonna come over and check out my new digs. On the corner of Stanyan & Carl, there was a Cala Foods grocery store and across from that was a likker store. I got some cheese, a big chunk of salami, two of them baguette bread things that were the latest rage, a bottle of Jose Takillya, a case of Miller Lite, limes and salt, and that was the fixins for my first party. I had to make 2 trips to carry it all. Oh,....and I still had some good green bud from my supply which was still holding out,...but just barely.

When Steve rode over that afternoon I heard his Shovel pull up below so I ran down the stairs and opened the garage door for him to roll his bike inside. Pretty fuckin' classy of me, huh? While we ate and drank and smoked standing up cuz I ain't got any chairs or bed to sit on, I told him I had to leave again to go back up to Wenatchee Washington, so don't freak out cuz I ain't dead again, wink, wink.

When I got ready to go back to Washington, I grabbed my little road bag with clothes and weed and caught a cab that took me to the SF Airport. I simply walked up to the counter and told the gal I wanted a one way ticket to Seattle. She punched some keys, and there was my ticket and she told me which gate to go to. Imagine doing that today? The flight to Seattle wasn't very long at all and this was only the 2nd time I had ever been in a commercial plane. And if you've ever been to the Sea Tac Airport up by Seattle and Tacoma, it's kind of a pain in the butt if ya ask me, cuz it ain't in either city. Ya gotta take a tram ride in to the main airport building if you're headed to Seattle, and from there catch another bus that takes you to downtown Seattle, in the scummy part of town where the Greyhound Bus Station is,.....or was back in 1983. Probably all fancy million-dollar condos today, hah.

By the time I got to the Seattle Greyhound station, the guy told me the last bus for Wenatchee had already left, so now I'm stuck in the Greyhound station for overnight. The cops there will not let you sleep on the benches, lyin' down, anyhow. So I had to sleep on the fuckin' bench sittin' up, taking little cat naps. Around 6:00 the next morning, their cafe finally opened up in the station and I had me some good coffee and donuts. Finally, the bus was ready and took me and a few other toads over the pass to Wenatchee, stopping at little towns along the way, of course, hahaha. It was a Milk Run. Geeze. When the bus finally dumped my sorry ass off in Wenatchee, now I was hoofin' it, no wheels at all. And I don't remember if I ever even saw a cab the whole time I lived in Wenatchee.

I finally made the walk to the U Haul place and got their smallest truck they had for rent. Mind you, I did not have a credit card. If I remember right, I gave them like a 200 bucks deposit which I got back at the end of the move. I drove my new U Haul wheels over to the storage unit and loaded the truck. After I tied everything off good and the truck was ready, I drove by my Wenatchee friends' places to puff, drink, and say good bye again. Then I headed back over Blewett Pass for what seemed like the 4,938th time, haha. I stopped by Dane & Stacey's and saw them and their two little girls and their dog. They even had another Unemployment Check there waiting for me,...yay! See how that happened? My 3 State Interstate Claim was based in San Francisco, and the SF Office mailed my Unemployment Check 850 miles up to Ellensburg Washington and then I drove up there to get it and bring it back to Frisco to stick it in my new bank account. Crazy, eh?

When I got ready to leave this time, I decided to try a different route just to see some new shit, ya know? So I went the more interior way, down the eastern side of Oregon on Highway 395. I saw all kinds of new interesting sites. And dammit, the one thing I forgot to pack on this trip was the Canon camera, hah. It was back in Frisco, so I ain't got no pictures of this part of the trip. I stayed on 395 South all through Northern California, too, cutting over by Sacramento and then finally to the Bay Area. I got two motels this time cuz I got started the trip in the middle of the day and this route took longer to make, like three days instead of two.

When I got back to Frisco I unloaded the U Haul. That means I carried everything up all those dang stairs, hah. I hooked up the Technics stereo first thing, and laid the albums out in 4 stacks about 3 feet long each stack. See there? I told you I was a music freak, ha ha-ha, and I had a row of albums probably 12 feet long and I kept them all in alphabetical order, just like a record store would do. Cuz otherwise,...how would you ever find the one you're lookin' for? I got the truck totally unloaded then drove it down to Dudley Perkins on Page Street and got my ol' carpenter toolbox buddy from the storage unit, rolled it up the U Haul's ramp and got it back to the flat, stuck it in the garage with the chopper. YAY! This is the first time I have had everything together, in the same state mind you, since the summer of 1981 when I went berserk and homeless.

Next up on the agenda was the blacksmith. The what,... you say? I said the blacksmith. James Perkins down at Dudley's looked at my Emergency Road Repair on the once beautiful frame neck and he suggested I put a bigger gusset in there to strengthen it all up. I asked him if he wanted to do it. He said he'd love to, but they were swamped with work. Then he told me "You can take it down to the black-smith on Harrison Street by the Oakland Bridge and they can fix it for you." I said, "BLACKSMITH? Here in San Francisco? You got a blacksmith here in town?" He said yep, told me where it was and that's where I went. The blacksmith cut out a rough gusset and welded it on there, so now it's a REAL rat bike chopper.

Oh, and there's more bad shit. The nice one piece chrome drag bars I had been running for a few years had the welds break loose, maybe from the wreck swith the VW Bug? Who knows?

Luckily for me, I had my younger brudder's old black handlebars from his 71 Shovel Chopper, and they were exact copies of the bars I had. And they are the very same black handlebars that I run today, except now they are chrome. So here ya go, behold the 'Newest Rat Chopper in The Haight'. This is my new blacksmith gusset and the black Dutch & George hand-me-down handle bars, sittin' in my new driveway on Stanyan Street. And now that frame neck is REALLY fucked up, hahaha.

Well, it's getting near the end of March 1983 and I got everything together and all situated in the rented flat in The Haight. So next I started looking for a carpenter job. No solid offers but I kept at it.

Meanwhile, I was riding the chopper around and exploring my new home town. I liked to ride over to North Beach, the old Italian part of the city which had also been home to the Beatniks and still had wonderful coffee houses, and by that, I mean coffee houses, not designer coffee boo-teaks like today. Chinatown was right next to North Beach, and then Pier 39 and the other less famous piers ran along the water front until ya got to the Golden Gate Bridge where the big ocean-going vessels floated in and out.

And the closest and most fun ride was right out my front door. Oh shit, and get this, I almost forgot to tell ya's, this flat I was renting here was also up on a hill, see? And that means I always got free starts riding down the hill and poppin' the suicide clutch. I'd ride down Stanyan and go past Haight Street, then turn left and ride through Golden Gate Park, and it was no helmet law back then. I'd ride through the giant trees and along the nice smooooooth road, and when I got to the end of the park, guess what was there? A big ol' windmill, yes, like from Holland and it was surrounded by a big ass tulip garden and then there was the Pacific Ocean with the waves coming in.

I'd ride to the ocean and smoke buds while the sun sank over the water. Not a bad life for a hobo newbie in town, eh? And one day while I was puffin' and watchin' the sun set, my mind flashed back to Wenatchee Washington and my ol' asshole buddy Washington State Patrolman Truman Douglas, bwah a ha-ha. The joke really turned out to be on his stinky ass. I made a clean getaway and there was not one damn thing he could do about it now. He thought he was sooo fuckin' smart, always tryin' to force me to try to get a Washington license tag. I was onto his game. Ya see, he didn't really want me to HAVE a Washington license tag, he wanted me to TRY and get one. Then while he was doing the State Inspection, he could say he found something 'suspicious' on the chopper and impound it.

Sometimes they'd keep a guy's bike for a week or two, and one guy I knew had his bike impounded for a whole fuckin' year, and when they finally gave it back to him, it was in boxes, and it had been a running Panhead that he had just restored and was trying to get the license tag for. So if they impounded my bike, too, then what the fuck would I have done? Been stuck there walking? That's why I rode back to Dallas to get a new license tag sticker, and since I am the original owner of the 74 Shovel, that means I still have the original paperwork from the dealer. So I had the upper hand on ol' asshole Truman Douglas. I hope that turd is in an old folks home right now poopin' his drawers and has tape worms. He deserves it.

But the Washington State Patrol Officers in Ellensburg were decent folks and they gave me a Washington tag and title with no problem, plus I even got a Washington State driver's license there. So here I am, finally with their Washington license tag and paper work after them assholes tried to make me get it for 3 years, but I am flying that white & green Washington tag in California, hahaha! This here is a picture of the 74 Shovel Chop on the next page, up on a nearby hill on Ashbury in the Haight looking out at the Pacific Ocean.

After the middle of March comes the end of March and that was also the end of the nervous and free wheelin' and miserable and funny Chopper Hobo Life for me. In other words, I finally got a fuckin' job, hah. I started in working for a classy construction company called Western Woodcraft, now defunct, RIP. They had their own big cabinet shop that had maybe 15 to 20 guys working and I was on the outside being an installer, which was fine with me.

The Koa wood toolbox was a semi-smash hit with the owner of the company and maybe that's how I got in, cuz I sure as hell didn't know anybody and I'm guessing it wasn't my stunning Sasquatch looks that got me hired, hah. The best thing about this job was I met my future main ridin' partner, Dave the guy who originally built the 67 Shovel Chopper which I eventually got from him in February 1989.

So now I was gonna get a regular pay check coming in, and I mean a real one that was made outta real paper that you actually took to the real bank. Weird, eh? I was still riding with Oakland Steve. He told me about a cool ass campground north of Frisco called Ring Canyon Campground, right in the middle of the Armstrong Redwood Forest & Park. For only 5 measly bucks you got a camp spot in the middle of the Redwoods, and they even had showers. The ground was mostly dirt, but they did have nice permanent rock fire pits. They also had these wooden lockers built there at each camp site to store your stuff in to keep the critters out.

Granted, I had no idea this Ring Canyon Campground even existed, and Steve may have been treating me like he was the Experienced Tour Guide and I was the dumb tourist, but once we got there, Steve found out just who it was that knew their way around a fire pit and who could grill up T Bone steaks, corn on the cob and stash baked taters in aluminum foil down in the coals, ha ha-ha. We had fun drinkin', tokin'. eatin', and ridin' through them big trees, too.

As for the 74 AMF Chopper? It went from a show bike quality Chopper to Rat Chopper in three years, and it continued to rat out. It hit runs in the Bay Area, up and down Highway 1 and 101, that September it caught on fire out in the desert in Needles California and I didn't even know it until I pulled into a gas station and shocked all the customers, hah. After the back end burnt up then it looked even worse. I kept riding it into the late 1980s, Redwood Runs and such, then moved to Seattle July 1, 1988.

By that time, the 74 Shovel Chopper was an oil slingin' fishtail smokin' 100% certified rat bike chopper. I tore it apart in a 1 bedroom apartment in Seattle, cut off the bad frame neck at the seat post and foot pegs areas,..again,....and took the motor and tranny to Northwest Custom Cycle for a rebuild. The guy who owned the shop was also named Dave, hahaha. This is gettin' corn-fusin', ain't it? When he got the motor apart, I polished up the cases on the engine and tranny.

While that was going on, in February 1989 right outta the blue my Frisco carpenter/ridin' buddy Dave with the 67 calls from Frisco and tells me his back went bad, he had just gotten a Softail and is putting his 67 Old Yellow up for sale. I panicked, asked him how much, he said 4,500, so I sent Dave a cashier's check from the 2 grand I had saved up for my engine and tranny bill and then I took a bus down to Frisco, gave Dave the other 2500 on a credit card cash advance (see what happens when they let me have a credit card?) and then I rode the 67 back up to Seattle,...in the rain and snow. It was a miserable two day ride.

Then, on April 1, 1989 the Northwest Custom Cycle shop burnt to the ground, with the 74's motor and tranny in it. So it had to be rebuilt again and I hadn't even gotten it back the first time yet. We moved back down to San Francisco September of 1989 just in time for the 7.1 Earthquake in October, nice eh? I still had the Old Yellow 67 to ride around Frisco while the 74 finally got finished and then I fired it up November of 1990, took me 1 year and 10 months to finish it, in two states.

At Dudley Perkins 1990 Toy Run it got 'discovered' by the guy who ran the Cow Palace Motorcycle Expo, and he invited me to show it there,...so I did. The 74 AMF is now silver blue and back to show condition and hits the runs and goes camping at the 1991 Redwood Run. Moved back up to Seattle just after the '91 Redwood Run. Stuck the 74 AMF in the Seattle Autorama that fall where Ed Roth and the Easyriders guys were there with their World Speed Record Streamliner. They also liked the 74 Shovel Chop and asked if I wanted it in their magazine. So I did that, too. Total of 3 Autoramas and 2 ER BIke Shows, more runs, then changed the bike a little bit, then moved to Wisconsin in July, 1995. At the Easyriders Bike Show & Rodeo in Milwaukee 1996, the 74 AMF Chopper got to park in between their Captain America and Billy Bike and I rode it to the Harley Birthday Bashes and Rat Rod events. It lives in the garage now right next to the now Rat Fink Green 67 Shovel Chop that it rode next to, back in California in the 1980s.

I will now leave you with some parting photos from back then and today. First, we have the Black Busted 74 AMF Rat Chop on the sidewalk at the flat in the Haight, March 1983. And then this might well be the first ever Chopper Hobo Fashion Show, that's right, here's what the Chopper Hobo wore back then. On the far left side we have the Heavy Duty Cold Weather Line, there is the original 1975 AMF Leather Jacket, and then the Ellensburg Chaps, with the 1977 Easyriders magazine Nasty Feet Boots, and up above all that mess is the leather Flying Ace hat and goggles with heavy gauntlet gloves. In the middle we have the Medium Duty Spring and Fall Line, featuring that Buckskin Fringe Jacket I got at the base of Pikes Peak in 1973 and the dog slobbered chewed up Harley sock hat with medium weight gloves. On the far right side is the Light Weight Summer Line, vintage Frisco Choppers T Shirts and my old 1982 Dudley Perkins Bandana, which used to be black.

And last but certainly not least, we have The Star of all this shit show that made it all possible, a-hangin' right there on the handlebars. Ladies and gentlemen, feast your peepers on the 1979 Canon AE-1 Camera that took all the fuckin' photos all those years ago and always got me 50 clams from the hock shops when I was broke. And it still works.

My Shovelhead brother Oakland Steve passed away in 1991, too soon at the age of 36, and on Page 53 in the August 1993 issue of Easyriders mag, I dedicated the Silver Blue build to him. I'm 67 now and yes, I'm still riding it and still building choppers and I still wear that dog slobber sock hat from Ellensburg, 1983. Some hobo habits never change.

THE END